Is Day Care Still at the Cross Roads?

of related interest

Day Services for People with Learning Difficulties
Edited by Philip Seed
ISBN 1 85302 339 6

Handbook for Assessing and Managing Care in the Community
Philip Seed and Gillian Kaye
ISBN 1 85302 227 6

Introducing Network Analysis in Social Work
Philip Seed
ISBN 1 85302 034 6 hb
ISBN 1 85302 106 7 pb

Social Work in the Wake of Disasters
David Tumelty
ISBN 1 85302 060 5

Dementia
New Skills for Social Workers
Edited by Alan Chapman and Mary Marshall
ISBN 1 85302 142 3

Is Day Care Still at the Cross Roads?

Philip Seed

Jessica Kingsley Publishers
London and Bristol, Pennsylvania

The right of Philip Seed to be identified as author of this work has been asserted by him in accordance with the Copyright, Designs and Patents Act 1988.

First published in the United Kingdom in 1996 by
Jessica Kingsley Publishers Ltd
116 Pentonville Road
London N1 9JB, England
and
1900 Frost Road, Suite 101
Bristol, PA 19007, U S A

Copyright © 1996 Philip Seed

Library of Congress Cataloging in Publication Data
A CIP catalogue record for this book is available from the Library of Congress

British Library Cataloguing in Publication Data
Seed, Philip
Is Day Care Still at the Crossroads?. -
2Rev.ed
I. Title
362.220941

ISBN 1-85302-373-6

Printed and bound in Great Britain by
Athenaeum Press Ltd, Gateshead, Tyne & Wear

Contents

Preface

The first edition of *Day Care at the Crossroads* was published in 1988. It was the culmination of a wide-ranging evaluation of day services for people with learning disabilities undertaken in Scotland between 1985 and 1987. Apart from a number of area conferences in Scotland, the research findings and recommendations were disseminated in shorter written forms, including a *Summary Report* published by the Scottish Office and illustrative *Case Studies* published by Jessica Kingsley. Particularly influential also was the Preliminary Report published by Costello in 1986 under the title *Which Best Way?*

While some of these materials are still available in their original forms, I am aware that many concerned with the running of day services are searching for the kind of guidelines that came from the study in a form which is shorter than the first edition of *Day Care at the Crossroads*. Hence this updated summary which takes into account the implementation of the National Health Service and Community Care Act 1990 and – more generally – a changed economic and social culture.

Is Day Care Still at the Cross-Roads? is also written in response to a continuing need for staff training materials. In particular, it is a recommended text for use with a study course published in 1995 by the British Institute for Learning Disabilities.

In deciding what to include and what to leave out from the original research reports, I have kept a considerable number of short case studies. These are intended for use in formal training as well as to help practitioners to reflect informally on their current work.

As a further aid to training and reflection, the main text is interspersed with questions about current practice, indicated by broad arrows.

The Introduction to *Day Care at the Crossroads* noted three major things that had happened during the preceding 15–20 years:

1. There had been an expansion in the scale of provision of day care and a corresponding expectation that, whatever day care was, it should be provided.

2. The acceptance of wide-spread unemployment in society had brought about a liberalising effect on the role of day centres by encouraging diversification of policies and practice.

3. A wind of change in the form of a broad international movement concerned with care in the community had swept away a lot of ideas and practices and was beginning to provide some of the answers to the questions that had been raised about the role of day services. Yet these answers had been mainly in terms of pioneering projects here and there rather than in terms of standard practice.

The book concluded with the alternatives of direction clearly facing day services at that time:

> One way leads to expansion of numbers, low throughput, centre-based activities, an emphasis on respite to parents and (if possible) constructive rather than meaningless occupation for the sake of it. This consolidates the role of day centres in offering centre-based activities away from educational institutions and favouring stability in a client's pattern of living. The client derives satisfaction from pretending to be at work while the parent gets respite and the tolerability of the home situation for both parties is sustained.
>
> The alternative road challenges the assumptions of centre-based activities. It looks instead at effectively increasing the educational component and, as this is accomplished, the patterns of living for the client are likely to change. *The key policy and practice issue is whether we want this to happen.* Do we want clients to think about leaving their parents? About getting married? About having children? About preparing for work? About retirement? Changes in family structure will occur in any case. Parents get older and die. If change is not planned by educational means, changes in family life will be seen as a series of crises calling for drastic intervention like admission

to long-stay homes or other institutions. The challenge is to prevent this. (p.287)

That was 10 years ago. How far has anything changed? Have day services gone down the second road to any significant extent? This book does not provide a definitive answer to these questions – that would require another large-scale piece of research. Instead it offers practitioners and managers the means to answer the questions for themselves so far as their own operations are concerned. In considering the aims and results of day centres, maybe we can each find part of the answer to the basic question, *Is Day Care Still at the Crossroads?* and move on from there.

CHAPTER ONE

What are Day Services for?

Between 1985 and 1987 the author led a team of researchers evaluating day services in Scotland. After a survey of the main features of 92 local authority centres throughout Scotland, a sample of 146 users and their carers was drawn from 15 centres replicating the features of the larger sample.

The long deliberations about which centres to select led to the formulation of seven models of practice, first described in *Which Best Way?* (Seed *et al.* 1984). These were:

- The Work Model
- The Social Care Model
- The Further Education Model
- The Assessment and Throughput Model
- The Recreational Model
- The Shared Living Model
- The Resource Centre Model[*]

It must be stressed these were models in the sense of definitions or key descriptions of practice that were found at that time. They were not models in the sense of practice that we were recommending. Their purpose was to provide a framework for evaluation. Which model fared best?

The answer was not a simple one – it depended on how aims of centres were perceived and this, in turn, depended on whose

---

[*] A summary outlining the details of each of these seven models will be found in the Appendix.

perspective we were mainly considering – the perspective of client, parent, professional or management?

When, during the early part of the research, we interviewed senior management, we found the following aims to be associated with each of the seven models:

1. **The Work Model** – to provide work experience and, where possible, preparation for employment.

2. **The Social Care Model** – to provide social education, i.e. to develop normal living potential and social skills needed in a family and community context.

3. **The Further Education Model** – to provide continuing education to develop adult potential.

4. **The Assessment and Throughput Model** – to channel people to more appropriate (more normal) placements including preparation for employment.

5. **The Recreational Model** – to provide opportunities to develop individual potential through a range of interests and activities.

6. **The Shared Living Model** – to provide opportunities for shared learning.

7. **The Resource Centre Model** – to meet a variety of client and community needs, as a resource centre.

> *Which, if any, of the above descriptions of aims comes nearest to the way management perceives the aims of current day services? If the answer is some combination – for example 1, 2 and 3 – how far are these aims compatible? Are there any conflicts between the priorities given to different activities?*

These were the views of management. We also asked other staff for their opinions as well as parents and the day-service users themselves.

We found that parents and staff largely coincided in their views on three broad aims and that these aims applied, so far as they were concerned, for all centres largely independently of the particular model of practice that we ascribed to each centre:

- 90% of parents and staff approved of centres aiming to help the client to live more independently and to have basic *survival skills*.

- 75% of parents and staff approved of centres aiming to provide social activities.

- Over 60% of parents and staff thought that centres should fulfil a respite function for parents or other carers at home.

However, the general convergence of views in favour of these three aims contrasted with a divergence of views, both between parents and staff and also amongst parents and staff on two other aims:

- The first was helping the client to find a job – 28% of parents approved of this aim compared with 64% of staff.

- Second, there was disagreement as to whether the aim of centres was simply to provide occupation – 49% of parents approved of this as a legitimate aim compared with only 11% of staff.

> *How far do staff and parents (or other carers) share the same understanding of the aims of your day service? How many parents would today think the aim of your centre was to help the client find a job?*

Early on in the research, clients were asked about centre aims in a slightly different form. They were asked why they thought they came to the centre. One-hundred-and-twenty-one clients were interviewed and asked to respond to a number of possibilities.

The largest number of positive answers was clustered round the idea of attending a centre in order to make friends. Seventy six said they came to make friends while two said this was not why they came.

The second largest group of answers was clustered round the idea of learning. Fifty nine said they came to learn while and six said they did not come for this.

The third group of answers clustered around the idea of finding a job. Thirty-two gave positive answers for this and 10 said this was not why they came. Thus, as with parents and staff, preparation for work was a controversial aim. If anything, it represents a higher proportion of clients approving of this as an aim than expressed by parents. The question was difficult for some clients to answer because they perceived attendance at the centre as *going to work*. We discovered that in many cases this view was promoted by parents and, to a lesser extent, by staff. The idea was reinforced, for some, by the fact that they received a nominal payment for going to the centre.

Why do clients or service users think they attend? How many think they come to train for future employment? How many see attending the centre itself as their work?

Are the answers to these questions affected by what you call service-users (trainees, clients, students etc.?) or by payment, if any, received for attending?

If we combine these various perspectives, including the views of management on which our original seven models of practice were based, the answers to the question *'What are centres for?'* can be summarised as follows:

1. Centres have a broad aim to develop the clients' potential. This implies that clients attend in order to learn something. It is a general educational aim which different models of practice will interpret with particular slants – for example, in the case of the work model the emphasis is on the potential for work while with the recreational model the emphasis is on sport and leisure pursuits.

2. Preparation for more independent forms of living. All models of practice subscribe to this, tending to see their particular slant as the means to its attainment. Thus work is a means to greater independence because being at work offers a more independent status. Developing the capacity for recreational

activities also enhances status and in general gives confidence. Preparation for independent forms of living is central to the social care, further education, resource centre and throughput models.

3. Positive throughput – that is, clients are expected to move on. It regards attendance at centres as temporary and a specific preparation either for work or for some other positive purpose outside the centre. This has particular significance for the work, further education, throughput and resource centre models. It will be considered as appropriate perhaps for only a minority of clients in the social care model. It is not necessarily an aim at all in the recreational model.

4. A general aim of enriching the clients' patterns of living (quality of life) at home. This applies particularly to the social care and resource centre models and it applies least, if at all directly, to the work model.

5. To provide social activities and opportunities for mixing amongst clients at centres. Although this was not stressed to us as an aim by management it cannot be ignored in view of the high priority it is given by parents and clients and to some extent by staff. It is perhaps particularly applicable to the social care, recreational and shared living models. It may also be applicable, in a slightly different sense, to the resource centre model. It features incidentally, but not as an aim, in other models.

6. To provide respite for parents or other carers at home. We found controversy in considering how this fits into other aims but there is no doubt it is an aim, especially for centres closest to the social care model but also (in some cases) for most other models except the work model.

7. Finally there is a specific aim associated with the resource centre model – namely to be a resource for clients, their families and the wider community including those who are helping to facilitate people with learning disabilities to live more normal lives and even, in some cases, specifically to manage in a house or flat away from their parents.

Some of these aims were, and still will be, controversial. Do you think people's views have changed during the past 10 years?

Some centres today are called Resource Centres. *What does this mean?*

CHAPTER TWO

Some Examples of Centres in 1985. How Much has Changed?

The wide variety of day services is illustrated in the following examples from the original survey. Here *small* means up to 40 users, *medium* between 40 and 75 users and *large* over 75 users.

Centre 14

This service was designated as a work centre rather than as an adult training centre and aimed to provide or to find employment. All users had to be able to travel independently to the centre. There was approximately a 1:5 instructor to user ratio.

It was a small centre, recently re-located on the edge of an industrial town but in a residential area. It shared old buildings with a special school for children with severe and profound learning disabilities. A lodge had been modernised and was being used as a domestic training unit. The hall of a nearby adult training centre was used for sports activities. Some users attended work placements outside including work in a home for the elderly and in a social work office.

Activities at the centre included labelling tie hangers, assembling light fittings, making soft toys and operating a small printing press. There was also gardening and woodwork. The manager was involved in the management of a range of residential and field services in the area.

This centre was closest to the work model. It was unusual at that time in being so specialist in this respect. It encountered two main problems. The first was the shortage of employment opportunities and the second was the absence of any mechanism for dealing with issues or problems relating to carers or to the users' home situations. Was the model wrong, or the methods?

Centre 12

This was a fairly new purpose-built centre in a large city. It incorporated what was called *a profound unit* (for people with severe or profound learning disabilities, many of whom had additional physical disabilities or sensory impairments). It had a large catchment area since it was the only day service in this area which could cope with such people. It was situated on a housing estate and, although purpose-built, the building was not regarded as large enough.

The staff stressed the need to inform people of their welfare rights and parents were encouraged to come in to seek advice. There was a coffee bar in which users (who were called students) were involved.

Amongst the recreational activities offered there was an emphasis on swimming.

This centre included a wide age-range – older students being up to 65 – as well as a wide range of disabilities. It had a higher than average staff : student ratio on account of the profound unit. There was also a high staff turnover.

This centre, closest to the social care model, was trying to individualise aims for a wide range of different attenders. Who would lose out? What would you think could have been the reasons for a high staff turnover?

> *Is your centre purpose-built? Is it large enough? What criticisms do you have of the design? What advantages do you see in the design?*

Centre 19

This centre had a policy of explicit emphasis on the principles of normalisation. There was an emphasis on small groups including a social awareness group and sex education courses were offered. A small domestic training group involved trainees visiting each other's homes with an instructor. All staff attended parents' meetings.

Housed in a former school building, the centre served a large urban catchment area. The inadequacy of the building was recognised.

The service specialised in those whose skills had developed to some extent but who were not yet ready, for example, for employment. All users travelled to the centre independently. There was about a 1:7 instructor to user ratio (including the manager and deputy).

> *This centre could be expected to benefit from having a definite focus backed by ideas. Why would the building be regarded as inadequate? Would you prefer to work in this centre rather than Centre 12?*

> *What do you think of the idea of a group of centre users and staff visiting the homes of individual users in turn?*

Centre 21

This was a small, newly opened centre closely linked with local community learning disability teams. It was purpose built in the residential area of a small town in a rural community, adjacent to a park.

The main emphasis was on assessment and training for living. Facilities included a kitchen and training flat as well as a laundry room. There were close links with other services including the local college of further education. Some members attended college courses.

Users were called *members*. One member attended the local community centre for lunch. Two members attended a health education clinic. The wide range of members included some with physical disabilities as well as profound learning disabilities.

People from a wide range of services who spent part of their time in the centre included a physiotherapist, a speech therapist, a social worker and a family aid. The centre's regular staff included a lecturer seconded from the local college of education. Additional staff were employed for particular members, including 1:1 support in the case of someone with very special needs.

There was combined staff/parents/client participation in an Open University Course.

> *This centre had much more of an educational focus, coupled with individualised programme planning and the operation of community teams. Fairly unusual in 1985, are centres on this model more commonplace today? More recent visits to centres suggest they are, but how often does the rhetoric of phrases like 'individualised programme planning' fail to match the reality?*

> *So far we have come across a variety of terms used for people who attend day services: clients, users, students, members. What term does your centre use? Does the term reflect the role adopted in relation to the centre's purpose? – i.e. student implies adult education, while member suggests a sense of participation and belonging, as with a club.*

Centre 25

This was a small urban-aided project which had made an application for main line financial support. This was granted and the centre is still operating 10 years on. It was called a *project* rather than a *centre* and was substantially different from other services in that *workers* (as they were called) were admitted in small groups of six to eight to attend, in the first instance, a course which was time-limited although the time limit was not precisely specified at the outset. At the end of this course they were expected to be ready for employment or, if this was not possible, work experience or voluntary work outside. Continuing support was available and contact maintained when the period of training was completed.

The project was based in an old school building which also housed a number of other activities and projects. The emphasis was on treating the workers as adults and working closely with them. They were helped to plan their own diaries and given support in arranging a wide-range of outside opportunities for further education, work introduction and work experience. There was an emphasis on group discussions, sometimes with people invited from outside. Some of the projects in which the workers were involved were within the same building. All workers had to travel independently to and from the project which was staffed by a qualified teacher and a qualified social worker. Because of difficulties in finding employment opportunities, the focus of throughput had broadened to include community and voluntary work. A more general aim was also incorporated to broaden horizons through educational, recreational and daily living skills.

This centre had some novel features, perhaps the most radical being time-limited attendance. Associated with guaranteed throughput, was the idea of group rather than individual intakes of new students. What do you think would be the advantages and disadvantages of these ideas?

Centre 10

This was another urban-aided project which achieved main line funding. It was based on part-time rather than full-time attendance. Originally this was to allow more people to attend but came to be seen as offering positive benefits. Two groups attended on a flexible basis, usually for two days out of four each week. The fifth day was set aside for staff meetings and also for a drop-in service available to any of the users.

The centre was situated in an inner city area where, like Centre 25, it shared an old school building with other social work facilities and also with community education. A wide catchment area was catered for which otherwise was poorly served by other facilities. The centre was also closely involved in the local community, for example in connection with a local fair. It also organised workshops involving parents, staff and trainees. There were links with the local further education college. Some of the users were people who had refused to attend other centres.

The main thrust of the activities was directed towards supporting people in their own homes and in the community, including a number of users who lived on their own.

> *What are the expected benefits of part-time rather than full-time attendance? Are there any disadvantages?*

At several centres at that time the notion of fixed groups based on one instructor to 8–10 trainees was giving way to the idea of key workers or tutors with a group of users undertaking a range of activities appropriate to their individual needs. Assessment at most day services was tending to become formal. However, there was no national standardisation of assessment procedures being used.

> *How far down the road described in the paragraph above have centres with which you are familiar gone?*

> *Which of the examples of centres described in this chapter would be most in keeping with the aims of care in the community? Why?*

> *Which, if any, would you think most likely to feature good practice? Which, if any, would you think likely to feature poor practice?*

Have parents' views changed in the past 10 years? Which of the centres described above would parents be most likely to favour?

In which of the centres would users be likely to have most opportunities for shaping their own programmes?

CHAPTER THREE

Have the Clients Changed?

One hundred and forty six clients were selected on a random basis from the 15 centres studied in 1985–7. Comparisons with other studies at that time suggested they were a representative sample.

About half of the clients were under the age of 30, half over the age of 30 while 8% were over the age of 50.

Are there more elderly people attending centres today?

A number of different indicators were used to describe clients' support needs at home, at the centre and at different times during the study. At the start of the evaluation:

- 80% could dress themselves without assistance or support: 69% could wash, bath and toilet.

- 85% could eat and drink without assistance or support.

- 87% were fully mobile.

- 90% had a vocabulary greater than 50 words.

- 62% could prepare a simple snack meal at home without assistance.

- 25% (only) could manage money without support or assistance.

- 54% could cope with public transport on their own.

How do these figures compare with clients' support needs in your centre today?

Fifty-nine (40%) of the 146 people in the sample were living at home in two-parent households. A further 35 (24%) were living in one-parent households – in 26 instances they were living with mother, in nine instances with father. In 14 cases people were living without parents but with their brothers or sisters. Twenty-one (14%) were living in hostels – a proportion which appeared to be representative for Scotland as a whole when the research began – and 6 in staffed flats (with at least a bedroom, sitting area and cooking facilities). Nine were living in un-staffed accommodation on their own or with other clients.

Nineteen (13%) in the sample came from family households where another member of the family was known to have attended a special facility for people with learning disabilities. In two cases this was a parent, in ten cases a brother or sister and in seven cases another relation.

About one third of clients had either left home or had been in long-term care and were now living in supported or unsupported accommodation in the community. How does that compare with the figure for your centre today? What are some of the implications for changes in these respects?

A majority in the sample, namely 84 (58%) were in living situations where they did not have access to the use of private cars.

Car ownership has increased since 1985 but is lower in some localities in Scotland than elsewhere in most of the UK. It is still false to assume that all households have cars. What are the implications for day service programmes? What are the implications for transport arrangements affecting clients attending centres today?

Sixteen clients had never been to school. Of the 130 who had been to school, their different types of schooling history was as follows:

Ordinary primary classes	67
Ordinary secondary classes	19
Special primary schools or classes	98
Special secondary schools or classes	94
Private day schools	7
Residential special schools	8
Hospital schools	7

At first sight it may seem the above figures show a surprisingly large number of then-current day service users had been to ordinary schools. The explanation is that older people were sent to their local school in the days before special schools had been developed in many localities.

Since 1985 much has been said about integrating people with disabilities into mainstream schools. Has this happened to an extent where the above figures would be affected?

Is there any evidence in your area that people with learning disabilities who attended ordinary schools found other opportunities for day-time activities outside centres?

Long-stay hospitals for people with learning disabilities featured in the past history of residential periods away from home (more than five days) in 21 instances. General hospitals featured in 60 instances – although in many cases more than one general hospital was attended by the same person. Seven people in the study had been in children's homes. Hopefully this would not be the case for younger people attending day centres today. On the other hand, we can expect a larger proportion of adults discharged from hospitals living in forms of adult residential care.

> *With the growing momentum of care in the community, has the proportion of people with a background in long-term care increased in your centre? If this is the case, what are the implications?*

After leaving school and before attending their present centre, 32 people in the study (22%) had been in open employment, three had been in sheltered employment and three had taken part in other work experience. Eight had attended colleges of further education before coming to their present centre, but by far the largest number (of those who had not come to their present centre straight from school), namely 67, had come from other adult training centres.

> *Numbers in open employment at some time before coming to the centres were surprisingly high. What would be the likely proportion today? What are the implications?*

The following are examples of the social backgrounds of four clients, picked at random from the 1985–7 sample:

Jack (aged 28)

Jack lived alone with his 68-year-old mother in a council flat. His father had died a year before the start of the study. They had no car but lived near several bus routes and the shops were only two minutes' walk away. Jack attended three separate special schools. He was not happy at school and his mother was bitter when he left because there was no place then available at a day centre. Previously she had been forced to fight to get Jack a place at a special school. She was told at that time that he was ineducable but she knew this was not the case and in fact demonstrated to a visiting inspector that he could, for example, set the table. They managed for many years without any services and she became accustomed to coping on her own. More recent studies have shown that there are still referrals to day services today on behalf of people who have had no previous services, especially people who have more severe learning disabilities than Jack appeared to have.

Jean (aged 30)

Jean lived with her mother and father in a second floor council maisonette. It was approached by steep steps which caused some problems for Jean. The nearest bus route was seven minutes' walk away as were the shops. When the study started her mother was working but her father was unemployed. The family car was off the road waiting for repairs. Jean had attended a junior occupation centre and thereafter she attended another adult training centre until she moved, just before the study started, to her present day centre. She had no past history of living away from home. The family often took their holidays when Jean was away on a centre holiday to Butlins.

Mary (aged 46)

Mary was brought up with her parents and attended an ordinary primary school followed by secondary special schooling. After her mother died and her father remarried she spent a short period living with another relation and then moved to a local authority hostel where she now lived. These various changes meant that Mary had attended several different day services. She had a slight physical disability making it difficult for her to climb stairs.

Alice (aged 37)

Alice lived with her elderly father and housekeeper. The father had moved specially to the town because he approved of the particular day centre there. They previously lived in a city where Alice was a day patient at a long-stay hospital. After her mother's death she attended hospital on a residential basis but the father was so concerned that Alice was not happy there that he made the present arrangement. When Alice was a child they had lived in England where Alice had been able to attend a private school.

Are these kinds of backgrounds familiar today? If not, what has changed and what are the implications?

A large majority (78%) of the clients had attended their present centre for less than six years. Fifty-two (36%) had attended for less than two years.

This finding reflected the expansion of day care services during this period. At the other end of the scale, eight people had attended for between 11 and 20 years and two people had been at the present day centres for over 21 years. These figures included breaks in attendance. Fourteen (10%) had taken breaks lasting more than three months for the reasons shown below:

Sickness	3
Further Education College	3
Sheltered employment	2
Work experience	2
Another Day Service (ATC)	4
Unemployed (at home)	4
Other	3
Total (including multiple answers)	**21**

These figures indicate the limited extent to which college courses, sheltered employment or work experience have been used in the past. The 14 who had taken breaks included eight who had been at the centre for less than six years as well as some of the very long-term clients. Two of the 14 were amongst those who had been at the centre between 11 and 20 years. None of those who had been in open employment before coming to the centre had subsequently had a break from attendance. Whatever the past reasons for failure in open employment, attendance at the centre appeared (at the start of the study) to have been regarded as permanent.

> *Is attendance at your centre today regarded as permanent? If not, where do you expect clients to move to, when, and for what reasons?*

Over half the clients in the sample had physical disabilities, illness, or sensory impairments other than a learning disability. The incidence of specific conditions was as follows:

Severe visual impairment	3
Severe hearing impairment	9
Epilepsy	18
Cerebral palsy	6
Mental illness or disturbance	7
Other physical disabilities	51

These figures illustrate the danger of overlooking aspects of people's needs, other than a learning disability. This is certainly as true today as it was in 1985. Often, indeed, sensory impairments may go unnoticed or not be attended to. This has led the Royal National Institute for the Blind (RNIB) to develop a multi-disability consultancy service and a new specialist day service in Glasgow working with other day service staff to assess the needs of people with learning disabilities and visual impairments and work with the parents and their regular day services to develop individual programmes.

Fifty-nine per cent of clients were described by their parents or main support people as healthy, despite their disabilities. Thirty-four per cent were regarded as having minor health problems and eight per cent as having major health problems or suffering from chronic ill-health.

Does this profile of disabilities and health match the population at your centre today? If not, what are the main differences?

CHAPTER FOUR

Activities and Objectives

ACTIVITIES

It is interesting to compare what activities were provided in centres in 1985 and what happens today, ten years on.

The 1985–7 study grouped activities into eight main categories:

1. **Work Tasks** – 10% of all activities

   Contract work. Semi-skilled trade. Gardening. Work experience in the centre. Paid work experience outside the centre. Voluntary unpaid experience outside the centre. Woodwork.

2. **Domestic** – 10% of all activities

   Domestic tasks and domestic training.

3. **Educational** – 24% of all activities

   Reading, writing and numbers. History, geography and science. Current affairs. Singing and music. Sex education. Shopping and cafe visits. Learning to use transport. Basic play. Drama. Physical education. Language and communication.

4. **Sports and Games** – 20% of all activities

   Computer games. TV and radio etc. Swimming. Sports at the centre and elsewhere both outdoor and indoor. Other games. Disco etc.

5. **Crafts** – 14% of all activities

   Crafts and craft work. Art.

6. **Personal Care and Hygiene** – 5% of all activities
   Hairdressing. Baths, showers and toileting etc.

7. **Special Projects and Trips Out** – 7% of all activities.
   This category did not include shopping.

8. **Other** – 10% of all activities
   Fund-raising. Trainee meetings. Counselling. Group discussions. Other activities.

During the two year research period, work and educational activities were proportionately increasing. Arts, crafts and sports and games were decreasing.

   Activities varied with the models of practice. Half the activities of those in the sample attending the work centre were either work activities or sports and games. Only 2 per cent of activities at centres following the recreational model were work activities while 55 per cent of activities were sports and games. Domestic activities were fairly evenly dispersed throughout all kinds of centres. Educational activities varied between constituting 8 per cent at the work centre and 39 per cent at the centres following the throughput model. Crafts hardly featured at all at the work centre and at the centres closest to the throughput model. They featured most prominently in the social care and shared living models. Hygiene was only specified as an activity for those at certain models of centre practice, and was highest (12%) for the throughput model.

> *How do these patterns of activities compare with activities on at your centre (a) in 1990 and (b) today?*

The Table below shows the type of activities and the time given to them as found in the 1985 survey. (Spaces are left for you to complete your own figures, five and ten years on. These figures should make an interesting point of comparison.)

Type of Activities:

	1985 *(All centres)*	1990 *(Your centre)*	*Today*
Work tasks	10%	_____	_____
Domestic	10%	_____	_____
Educational	24%	_____	_____
Sports and Games	20%	_____	_____
Crafts	14%	_____	_____
Hygiene	5%	_____	_____
Special project and trips out	7%	_____	_____
Other	10%	_____	_____

OBJECTIVES

Activities can mean very different things for different clients at different centres. To explore this in detail we asked each member of staff concerned with each client to describe in some detail for each activity what their objectives or expectations were. A total of 2051 objectives was recorded for a total of 1160 activities in which a total of 127 clients participated during a monitored fortnight towards the end of the research. The findings revealed nine broad categories of objectives:

1. Task Oriented Objectives (11%)

These were objectives oriented to the task in hand rather than to the person fulfilling the task. Eleven percent of the total fell into this broad category. These were very evenly dispersed throughout the different models of practice.

2. Developmental Objectives (29%)

These were distinguished from task oriented objectives in that they were person oriented rather than activity oriented and most of them were in terms of developing particular aspects of the individual's potential. In this case the incidence averaged 29 per cent but ranged from 20 per cent in the case of the social care model to 42 per cent in the case of the shared living model.

3. Daily Living Objectives (15%)

This category was defined as relating both to the person and to the task and had to be in terms of its application to daily living situations. The total percentage was only 15 per cent with a range between 4 per cent (recreational model) and 20 per cent (throughput model).

4. Behaviour Correction Objectives (1%)

We had included this heading expecting that there would be significant scores particularly in the case of the social care model. In fact there were only 30 objectives in all listed within this category (1% of the total). The largest single incidence was 20 in the case of the social care model.

5. Social Objectives (16%)

Social objectives were those which focused on clients' relationships with other people. In this case the average was 16 per cent with a range between 10 per cent (in the case of the throughput model) and 28 per cent (in the case of the recreational model). The work model had a proportionately higher score. Twenty-one percent of all objectives for the work centre were in this category. Twenty-five per cent of the objectives for the resource centre model were social objectives.

6. Assessment (4%)

We had anticipated that there would be a much larger score within this category. The total percentage of scores was only 2 per cent with the range between 0 per cent and 6 per cent.

7. Non-Specific Objectives (20%)

This category related to objectives which were so broadly expressed or defined that it was impossible to say whether they related to the person, the activity, daily living or to any of the other specific categories. Twenty percent of the total fell within this category. They ranged between 11 per cent for the shared living model to 28 per cent for the social care model.

8. No Objectives (3%)

In some cases the staff explicitly stated that they had no objectives. In other instances staff did not specifically state this but were unable to give any objectives. The scores were fairly evenly spread throughout the centre models representing about 3 per cent of the total.

9. Other Objectives (2%)

Finally a category was allowed for other objectives which could not be categorised within any of the above. This accounted for about 2 per cent of the stated objectives.

The highest number of objectives for all models of practice, except the social care model, were developmental. In the case of the social care model the highest number were non-specific. In each case the highest number represented around a third of the total number of stated objectives. The second highest grouping of objectives varied more with different models. Twenty-one per cent of objectives for the work model were social; 20 per cent of objectives for the social care model were developmental; 18 per cent and 20 per cent respectively for the further education and throughput models were daily living objectives. Twenty-eighty per cent and 25 per cent respectively for the recreational and resource centre models were social objectives while 18 per cent of objectives for the shared living model were in terms of daily living.

Using these headings for activities and objectives, assess the objectives for one or more particular clients attending your centre. How does the general pattern of activities at your centre compare with the patterns suggested in the statistics quoted?

CHAPTER FIVE

What, if Anything, do Clients Learn at Day Centres?

Carers at home and staff at centres were asked in 1985 whether they could think of anything specific that the client had learnt during the preceding year.

Something learnt during the past year (% totals)

	View at home	Staff view at centre
Yes, definitely	40	35
Possibly	17	16
Probably not	10	11
Definitely not	31	25
Other answers	2	12
	100	**100**

The extent of agreement between home and centre reinforced the general finding that a little more than half of day service users either possibly or definitely learnt something during the preceding year, while at least 25 per cent had definitely not learnt anything.

Ask this question about some of the people attending your centre today. How do the answers compare?

There were major differences depending on the model of practice most closely adhered to. This prompted us to examine the practice for each model in terms of (i) activities (ii) objectives and (iii) progress clients had made. Small groups of clients were selected for detailed study and comparison.

1. THE WORK MODEL

Three clients were selected for detailed study. These all happened to be aged under 21. They were also relatively capable, being able to perform most self-management and some daily living tasks.

They were all engaged in similar activities – gardening, woodwork and other work or domestic tasks as well as sports and games. Sports and games were regarded as 'very important'. The overall objective of the centre was to prepare people for employment. None of them had found employment although, of the three, Client A appeared to be the most confident and potentially nearest that goal. Client B appeared to have a domestic situation which the centre felt was impeding his progress.

Client C was making less progress. One of the staff blamed this on the home situation but it also appeared that some of the objectives were less focused on a specific living and working situation outside than was the case with the others. Daily Living objectives featured more prominently for A and B than for C.

Instead there were more developmental objectives for Client C. There were also more social objectives where they were trying to do things to Client C in a more general sense. For example, staff wanted him to be more hygienic. They also wanted to improve his powers of conversation. If these were the objectives, one wonders whether a centre based on this model was the best place to achieve them? If the objective was to help him to wash his hands, was cleaning paint brushes the best activity to pursue in order to do this?

These three cases illustrate a dilemma in the case of the work model. The objective of finding employment is a specific one but the problems surrounding young people who are not in employment are wide-ranging, quite apart from having a learning disability. Any young unemployed person may well be lacking in confidence and may well become slovenly. The solution to these problems, according to the philosophy of the work model, lies in preparing for useful employment.

This appeared to have been successful in the case of Client A – according to the home based assessment. In the case of Client C, the centre did not appear to see work experience leading to outside work as an immediate possibility and there may have been a tendency to rationalise activities in terms of developmental or social objectives. Examples were to 'get confidence' (through games) or to learn 'normal conversation' (through woodwork).

If you are seriously pursuing the work model you really have to believe that all your clients can find employment. Perhaps it will be supported employment but if employment opportunities are not being pursued the centre may tend to slip into providing what the manager at a different centre called 'a working day' or 'an occupy-ing day'.

In some cases staff expressed anxiety for older members in the group (not selected for detailed study) for whom the prospects of employment seemed dim. Objectives for these clients tended to be stated more frequently in terms of task fulfilment. In all but one case, the main support person at home did not consider that anything had been learnt.

Look at the programme of activities for Client C below. Then consider the earlier statement that you really have to believe all your clients can find employment otherwise the centre may tend to slip into merely providing an occupying day. How might you improve Client C's programme?

An Example of a Client Attending the Centre Based on the Work Model
Client C – Male, age-group under 21

Activities	Objectives (as stated by staff)
Gardening	Enjoyment, variety Mixing with other trainees Learning to take orders from another instructor apart from his own
Woodwork**+	Confidence Learning to work with other people Communication – normal conversation
Domestic++	To transfer learning to be more thoroughly hygienic
Games competition at centre+	To help him to handle pressure To get confidence
Football++	Team work – To help trainees realise they're there to help each other
Cleaning paint brushes	To take responsibility Hope he will transfer the lessons to other hygiene standards such as washing hands

Key

*   Major activity – at least two full days or equivalent during monitored period

**   Main activity – at least half the time during the monitored period

\+   Activity described as *very important* by staff

++   Activity described as *crucially important* by staff

The outcomes, the identifiable areas of progress, in this case were as follows:

(i) Home-based Assessment

Recreational: Doing well at swimming.

General: Anything learnt? – No, nothing.

(ii) Centre-based Assessment

Helping at home.

Some progress in cleanliness, but has now deteriorated again.

2. THE THROUGHPUT MODEL

Two examples chosen for detailed study came from a large centre, which had evolved over a period of years from a more traditional form of practice. There was a wide spectrum of age, length of time at centre and performance in terms of self-care and daily living skills clients could accomplish.

Client A had a much wider range of activities than the examples discussed from the Work Model. Work experience featured in Client B's programme but not for Client A. The objectives appeared for both cases to be more specific than for the Work Model and there was some evidence of the objective taking precedence over the activity; that is a goal was set and an activity was chosen to achieve this goal rather than selecting the activity from a limited range of choices and then finding a reason for doing it. There was still some evidence of the latter, however, in the case of Client A. For example under 'shower skills' the instructor said 'we all do it'. However, in the case of Client A there appeared to be a sense of direction and priorities with the emphasis on improving basic education as a means to more independent living.

> *Which is more the common practice in your centre: (i) A goal is set and one or more activities chosen to attain it? (ii) An activity is selected from a limited range of choices and then a reason is found for doing it?*

Work experience did not feature in this case, presumably waiting until these basic skills had been learnt. There was a sense of optimism that improvement could be made and this was shared between the centre and the home.

Client B appeared to present something of a puzzle to the staff. Assessment featured as an objective in more than one activity. The home-based assessment of the centre was not very encouraging while one of the instructors implied that if they could teach him to be more independent at the centre he could copy this at home. Work experience at the centre cafe was seen as a means of enabling him to be more independent – 'If he can fill up a roll he can do it at home'.

An Example of a Client Attending the Centre
Based on the Throughput Model
Client A – Female, age-group under 21

Activities	Objectives (as stated by staff)
Basic education and word recognition*++	Everything – To learn very basic reading Remembering numbers
Taking someone out to coffee	To have responsibility for someone out Helping her development
Moving to music+	Marvellous at it
Music percussion, singing in the choir	Stimulates memory
Physical education	Hobby Physical exercise
Games	Enjoyment, leisure
Swimming	Hobby
Shower	Part of hygiene programme
Computer games, recognising numbers*+	To learn basic educational skills
Knitting	A leisure period using hands
Hairdressing	Enjoyment To do it on her own
Coffee morning	Enjoyment
Modelling for a hairdresser	To be helpful

Key
*   Major activity – at least two full days or equivalent during monitored period
**   Main activity – at least half the time during the monitored period
+   Activity described as *very important* by staff

++ Activity described as *crucially important* by staff

3. THE RESOURCE CENTRE MODEL

In the last few years a number of day centres have changed their names to resource centres. While not all of them necessarily follow the model we identified in 1985, there was one centre in the sample at that time closest to this model which people attended part-time.

Two people were selected for detailed study, Client A who was in his late 30s and Client B who was in his late 20s. Client B had a considerably greater learning disability than any of the examples we have considered previously. A characteristic of Client A, which illustrates the policy of this centre, was the extent to which he was engaged in activities either outside the centre or relating to people outside. This might also have applied to Client B but a note appears in several places explaining that he had refused to go out on one activity outside – namely to a bowling club. Some of the activities he was engaged in were substitutes for this. Assessments of progress referred to in both cases include an improvement in communication and confidence – in one instance reading and in the other instance conversation.

In this centre, a general objective was to strengthen daily life, that is on days when the client did not attend, as well as at weekends. There is some evidence that this happened. For example, in the case of B there were two references to home.

Watering plants was partly 'so he can relate to tasks at home' whilst sports are 'important for mum' because she wanted him to improve his health. There was an emphasis on social objectives – especially in the case of A – and this presupposed that clients have social needs which were not met outside the centre. In case B the parents stated that progress had been made with speech, adding 'it's being amongst others at the centre'. Most of the other clients attending this centre were fairly able, and Case B was an exception in this respect. There were no cases in the group where it was definitely stated that 'nothing had been learnt'.

An Example of a Client Attending the Centre Based on the Resource Centre Model
Client A – Male, age-group 35–40

Activities	Objectives (as stated by staff)
Music++	Something he likes, interest at home Something to give everyone to do
Handwork++	To interact with others
Quiz visitors from another centre++	Social interaction with others from a more able group Standing and status within the centre
Preparing questions for competition	To get him involved in external competition with other people
Attending further education college	To improve reading Status for attending college Encourage social interaction
Carpet bowls	(Staff not interviewed)

Key
* Major activity – at least two full days or equivalent during monitored period
** Main activity – at least half the time during the monitored period
+ Activity described as *very important* by staff
++ Activity described as *crucially important* by staff

Do some people attend your centre part-time? Does this result in activities during the days when they do attend being more focused on their assessment and learning needs? What is the centre doing to support clients on the days when they do not attend?

4. THE RECREATIONAL MODEL

Two clients whose lives were studied closely were attending the one centre in the sample closest to a Recreational Model. They were, in many respects, interchangeable with the clients attending the other kinds of centres discussed so far, for example, the work centre. But they were exposed to a very different set of experiences. Client A, for example was a man aged 20 with no work and no expectation of work. Almost all his activities revolved around sports and games in which, fortunately, he seemed to be interested. While the staff took pride in the fact that he was a good sportsman, the objective of sporting activities was, in general, to improve his confidence and his skills at mixing with other people. The outcomes were positive. His home-based assessment particularly claimed that he had improved in many respects.

Client B, on the other hand, was not so interested in sports. Yet she spent half the monitored fortnight doing this. The view was expressed at home that she was falling behind in basic education.

The comparison between these two cases indicated that an emphasis on sports and other recreational activities was a way forward in many respects for some clients but not for others. It suggested that in an area where there could be a choice of centres to attend, the pursuit of recreational aims by one centre would allow the possibility of a selection based on the potential of clients to gain by this means. However in an area where clients effectively had little or no choice of centre to attend, the exclusive pursuit of recreational objectives would have appeared to put some clients at a disadvantage.

An Example of a Client Attending the Centre Based on the Recreational Model
Client B – Female, age-group under 21

Activities	Objectives (as stated by staff)
Sports**++	Improve confidence Physical exercise Learn rules
Sports outings*++	Confidence, mixing To improve skills Indoor games*+
News discussion+	To encourage speech Mixing in groups
Craft*+	To improve skills

Activities	Objectives (as stated by staff)
Swimming	Staff not interviewed
Current affairs (at college)*++	To learn To develop and extend potential

Key

*   Major activity – at least two full days or equivalent during monitored period

**   Main activity – at least half the time during the monitored period

+   Activity described as *very important* by staff

++   Activity described as *crucially important* by staff

> *Is there any reason why these kinds of activities could not be carried out in normal community or sports centre surroundings? (It will be noted that this person did attend College for an activity not exclusively related to sports).*

5. THE SHARED LIVING MODEL

The models we have considered so far all tended to have a preponderance of more able users. Two centres closest to the shared living model tended to have clients with a full range of abilities. Here arts and crafts featured more strongly than in the models considered so far. The objectives tended to be developmental, in some cases quite specifically so, with staff using such phrases as 'developing fine control'. The two cases chosen (from different centres) had broad similarities yet the outcomes were different. The home-based assessment in Case B was positive and the parents said she had learnt the use of money. By contrast, in Case A the home-based assessment was at best 'the same' and at worst, in answer to the question *Anything learnt? – '*No'.

There is no immediate answer as to why this difference occurred but it can be pointed out that, particularly in Case A, the objectives were very ambitious. She enjoyed several of the activities she participated in but this did not mean she was necessarily learning either in terms of the goals that were set at the centre or in terms of parental or other expectations at home. She was expected to improve skills in art, crafts, domestic activities, swimming and gardening – quite a programme for anyone in educational terms. Client B, on the other hand, had learnt in terms of basic education – and this was the one activity which was missing from A's programme, at least during the monitored fortnight.

An Example of a Client Attending the Centre Based on the Shared Living Model
Client A – Female, age-group 30–35

Activities	Objectives (as stated by staff)
Art*++	Improve fine motor skills Encourage sense of colour To identify colours To improve visual ability To define aspects of sensory perception
Crafts*	Enjoys it To develop fine motor skills To develop sensory perception and colour
Jigsaws+	Develop perceptive powers Develop a self-interest i.e. pursuing a particular activity out of choice

Key

*   Major activity – at least two full days or equivalent during monitored period
** Main activity – at least half the time during the monitored period
+   Activity described as *very important* by staff
++ Activity described as *crucially important* by staff

6. THE SOCIAL CARE MODEL

The largest number of centres were (and perhaps still are) closest to the social care model. Activities and objectives tended to be wide-ranging. The expectations of learning were less pronounced than in the case of the shared living model. 'Enjoyment' featured more prominently in the objectives. Individualisation of objectives to respond to different user's needs was, in theory, a feature of the social care model and the examples illustrate the varied extent to which this was attained. In none of the examples were the outcomes outstandingly positive. This may reflect a lack of focus in differentiating priorities.

For example, Client A was trying to learn about colours, shapes, water taps, how to manage in domestic affairs, how to increase his vocabulary, pronunciation, observation, concentration, free choice, the outside world, independence, and learning to write his name. Meanwhile through plasticine he was 'to have ideas about what he wanted to do'. The outcome of all this was 'much the same', although he had learnt to try to mow the grass. This was for an activity (gardening) where the objective was apparently 'enjoyment'.

An Example of a Client Attending the Centre
Based on the Social Care Model
Client A – Male, age-group 25–30

Activities	Objectives (as stated by staff)
Plasticine	For ideas about what he wants to do
Gardening	Enjoyment
Writing	To learn to write his name First steps in education
Solving simple puzzles	To concentrate better Observation To learn about colours, shapes etc.
Snooker	Enjoyment
Domestic*++	To learn to look after himself and to develop his independence
Accompanied staff	To help him to learn about the outside world To bank & shop
Listen to records+	To give him a free choice
Practise speech on tape recorder	Better pronunciation To increase his vocabulary

Activities	Objectives(as stated by staff)
Domestic – laying table help in kitchen	To learn to manage more in the domestic area To differentiate between hot and cold, as when using water taps

Key

*   Major activity – at least two full days or equivalent during monitored period

**   Main activity – at least half the time during the monitored period

+   Activity described as *very important* by staff

++   Activity described as *crucially important* by staff

Are you always clear why you are doing what you are doing with each client?

Objectives in the case of Client B (shown below) were somewhat vague. It was not surprising that the home-based assessment, in answer to the question '*Has anything been learnt during the past year that is useful in daily living?*' was 'nothing'. It might indeed be an achievement for a woman to go into a workshop area varnishing assembled wooden kits if the objective was that kind of employment. But the main objective for activities as a whole was nothing of the kind. It was 'enjoyment'. If the purpose of an educational outing was 'to introduce her to places outside' one might have chosen somewhere else rather than another day centre.

An Example of a Client Attending the Centre
Based on the Social Care Model
Client B – Female, age-group 25–30

Activities	Objectives (as stated by staff)
Making tea and something to eat	To prepare her for later life To teach her skills
Group discussion	Encourage her to put forward ideas and speak up
Disco*	Enjoyment
Researching	Enjoyment

Activities	Objectives (as stated by staff)
Crafts – painting, by numbers	Enjoyment (usually she does the painting for someone) Concentration
Education – writing numbers	(Instructor not interviewed)
Educational visits to another ATC**	To see another centre and give her an idea about places outside
Sports training for a sports meeting+	Enjoyment Achievement – hope she may get medals
Varnishing assembled wooden kits	Enjoyment Achievement for a woman to go into a workshop area

KEY

*   Major activity – at least two full days or equivalent during monitored period

**   Main activity – at least half the time during the monitored period

\+   Activity described as *very important* by staff

\+\+ Activity described as *crucially important* by staff

Large and Small Centres in the Social Care Model

Centres closest to the social care model included the largest centre in the study and one of the smallest. Since an explicit aim within the social care model is individualisation we asked whether size was a factor.

> *To what extent is individualisation possible in your centre? Is this affected by the size of your centre? (Large: 75+ clients; medium: 35–74 clients; small: under 35 clients.)*

An Example of a Client Attending a Small Centre
Based on the Social Care Model
Client A – Female, age-group 35–40.

Activities	Objectives (as stated by staff)
Listening to music	Enjoyment
Watching High School sports	She likes to watch people doing things she cannot do herself
General tidying stacking chairs	Something she can do – when she is left and has to be occupied Lets her get the use of her hands and saves them stiffening up
Games*	Makes her use her brain – keeps it active
Watching more able trainees	She enjoys it She enjoys company Opportunity to be in a smaller group which she likes
Domestic work*	To try to get her to do some more things which might benefit her later on
Washing clothes**	To help her learn to do it for herself
Colouring a picture	Just something to get her to do
Knitting*	To get her to use her hands (exercises)
Gardening	To follow through the fact that she volunteered Encourage her to volunteer
Personal Hygiene*	To get her to do as much as she can for herself
Outing to cafe*	She enjoys it and it gets her out into the community
Games at community centre*	To get her moving She likes it
Video recording	Just leisure
Visit to another	To take her out so she can mix trainee's house* To take her out of herself

Activities	Objectives (as stated by staff)
Reading a book*	She likes to read To stop her from falling back at reading

KEY
*   Major activity – at least two full days or equivalent during monitored period
** Main activity – at least half the time during the monitored period
+   Activity described as *very important* by staff
++ Activity described as *crucially important* by staff

The implicit philosophy in determining this client's activities appeared to be noting what gave enjoyment and pursuing this. The result was a beneficial one because staff had time to notice what she wanted to do and were able to encourage her self-motivation to learn. The outcomes in this case were as follows:

(i) Home-based Assessment

At home: She wants to be more helpful than she used to be.

Recreational: Swimming – she is now floating on her back.

Social: She is talking to neighbours now. Education: She discusses current topic she is reading in the papers.

Confidence: She is much more confident and chatty. She used to be so quiet.

(ii) Centre-based Assessment

Hygiene: She cleaned her own teeth – this was learnt in hygiene.

Confidence: Yes, she can volunteer now.

> *What are the advantages and disadvantages of basing a programme of centre activities on what seems to be enjoyable? Would it be likely to produce beneficial outcomes for all clients? Why did it seem to produce beneficial outcomes in this case?*

7. THE FURTHER EDUCATION MODEL

The second largest group of centres studied were closest to the further education model. These centres varied in terms of size and the age range of service-users. One centre in particular contained a preponderance of younger people. At this centre, the range of ability was greater than at the other two centres. The following three examples were chosen from three different centres.

Two of the clients were young and the third was in her late 40s. The older woman and one of the younger clients were relatively able. The other younger client needed more support for daily living skills.

An Example of a Client Attending the Centre Based on the Further Education Model
Client A – Female, age-group 24–30

Activities	Objectives (as stated by staff)
Free choice – games+	Enjoyment Sense of achievement
Disco+	Enjoyment Oscillations Communication with other trainees (including Makaton)
Sports training at public track+	Preparation for sports day. Enjoyment
Jigsaws Enjoyment	Sense of achievement
Community outing+	If she moves into a hostel in the future I doubt whether any of her family would take her out so the outings will give her an opportunity to prepare for the future Learn shopping skills To see how she interacts with normal people
Speech therapy++	To help her to learn Makaton to communicate more She enjoys seeing someone who is experienced and trained in this area

Activities	Objectives (as stated by staff)
Work book as part of social skills*+	Give her a break from money and sums which she is terrible at Needs to learn about money for independent travel in the future
Crafts – embriodery+	Sense of achievement
Personal hygiene++	Probably the only time she has an overall wash
Watching TV	Enjoyment
Domestic training flat+	(Instructor not interviewed)
Work book*+	Learning more about numbers

Key

*   Major activity – at least two full days or equivalent during monitored period

**   Main activity – at least half the time during the monitored period

+   Activity described as *very important* by staff

++ Activity described as *crucially important* by staff

Client A had a wide range of activities not dissimilar from the examples chosen from centres closest to the social care and shared living models. The activities which were considered important focused on projects which could be considered educational in a broad sense. However, the objectives were more specific – for example speech therapy was considered crucial to help her learn Makaton so that she could communicate more and also to meet someone who was experienced and trained in this.

A link was made between this activity and communicating with others at the disco. The outcome was that her communication was considered to have improved both at home and at the centre. The overall progress, however, was not startling and in answer to the question *Has anything been learnt that is useful in daily living?*, 'No' was given both at the centre and at home.

An Example of a Client Attending the Centre

Based on the Further Education Model
Client B – Male, age-group under 21

Activities	Objectives (as stated by staff)
Craft	To follow instructions Concentration
Horticulture	Teach basic skills Work with others in group Improve numeracy, time, date etc.
Woodwork	Follow instructions Teach woodwork skills and use of tools Increase confidence Satisfaction in producing end product Co-ordination Concentration Behaviour as following instructions is difficult for this trainee
Makaton	To enable him to communicate
Basic education*+	To enable him to be more independent
Personal care+	Increase personal skills Clothes care Hygiene
Craft	Co-ordination Concentration Develop creative/sensory ability
Pottery	Gives variety and choice to craft field Trainee sees development of stages in creative work Develop fine motor skills
Speech++	To make use of speech To use and understand language Back up speech therapy programme Part of total programme for trainee's speech development, i.e. physical exercise plus speaking
Meal making*+	Survival cookery Independence Awareness of healthy diet
Articulation++	Improve ability to communicate Improve intelligibility of speech

Activities	Objectives (as stated by staff)
Baking*	Skill learning Likes food – enjoyment To produce finished article
Basic education+	To improve skills Independence
Time orientation	To develop concept of time To tell the time To learn the task
Ironing	Improving skills Prepare for future independence Self help

Key

*   Major activity – at least two full days or equivalent during monitored period

**   Main activity – at least half the time during the monitored period

+   Activity described as *very important* by staff

++   Activity described as *crucially important* by staff

The activities in the case of Client B were less dispersed and concentrated on work and educational activities. Nearly all of the objectives were educational and 'enjoyment' did not feature at all. The educational programme was intensive. There was a particular emphasis on communication, basic education and social skills. It was an ambitious programme but the outcomes did not show that a lot of progress had been made. The assessments at home and at the centre were somewhat different. He was seen as having made good progress at home and possibly in basic education. At the centre it was suggested only that he had learnt to swim.

An Example of a Client Attending the Centre
Based on the Further Education Model
Client C – Female, age-group 40–45

Activities	Objectives (as stated by staff)
Craft*	Relaxation Break from pressure of looking after a relative
Art	Develop technical skills such as doing a staine glass window creatively
Craft*+	To learn tapestry – she wants to do this Enjoyment She is good at it
Gardening	To do task well
Athletics meeting*	To give her the chance to partake in an activity she has chosen herself To allow her to get away from home circumstances for a day, a break from caring for disabled relation Participation in the community
Education*	Develop reading/writing skills
Domestic	To release possible tensions of home circumstances when talking to the instructor
Woodwork	Enjoyment Help her to learn to use basic tools such as a screwdriver
Discussion group	(Staff not interviewed)

Key

*   Major activity – at least two full days or equivalent during monitored period

** Main activity – at least half the time during the monitored period

+   Activity described as *very important* by staff

++ Activity described as *crucially important* by staff

Like the previous case, Case C did include *enjoyment* amongst the objectives. There was also reference to *satisfaction* from creative work. Staff were aware that this lady in her late 40s, who was fairly capable, looked after a relative and needed a break. This was referred to no less than three times and was spelt out in relation to attending an athletics meeting. The objective was stated to be 'to allow her to get away from home circumstances' for a day (break from caring for disabled relation). The activities and objectives indeed might suggest a social care rather than a further education model. Like the other further education cases, however, the objectives were more specific and purposeful than any of the examples taken from the social care model. This person answered her own questions about the home-based assessment. She said she had learnt money sums as well as a tug-of-war in recreation. The staff were more sanguine but recognised that she had difficulties at home.

This was an interesting case in that it threw an unusual light on the issue of respite. One usually thinks it is the carer at home who needs respite. In this case, the client was also a carer of others with different needs at home. This may not be so unusual though it can easily be overlooked because we tend to think of people as being either clients or carers, forgetting the reciprocal element in most family relationships.

SUMMARY OF CONCLUSIONS

The work model and the recreational model produced good results for certain clients but this presupposed in the former overcoming the credibility problem of finding work in the present economic climate and in the latter that clients were interested in the activities that went with recreation. Thus a client who was interested in sport thrived on a programme largely made up of sporting activities. Another client who was not interested in sport did not thrive so well. These kinds of centres had focused objectives in relation to their specific aims.

In contrast, the shared living model was not focused in terms of learning objectives. Practice in the social care model was varied and a smaller centre followed better practice than a large one. Practice in the educational model was more focused and challenging as well as producing more favourable outcomes in terms of what clients learnt at the centres which was of use to them outside.

> *In pursuing educational objectives for service-users, how far is practice focused, challenging and producing more favourable outcomes than in the past?*

CHAPTER SIX

People with Profound Learning Disabilities

Most of the people attending day centres whom we considered in the last chapter were able to manage personal self-care tasks such as dressing, feeding, washing and going to the toilet, with a minimum of support. Their main need for support and training related to what we call daily living: shopping, crossing the road, preparing a snack and so on.

In this chapter we ask about learning in the case of the minority of day service users whose needs are much more pervasive and embracing. We refer to these clients as people with profound learning disabilities. Many, but not all, people with profound learning disabilities also have physical disabilities and/or sensory impairments. Out of the total sample of 146 only eight clients were in this category. There would be a higher proportion today, some in special units and others in separate specialist centres. In 1985, a larger proportion were in day centres run by voluntary organisations in Scotland. Some of these services have since been taken over by local authorities.

Six of the eight were in centres closest to the social care model. Of the remaining two, one was in a centre closest to the further education model and the other closest to the shared living model.

Client A attended a centre closest to the further education model. There was an intensive programme of activities aimed at stimulating and developing physical, intellectual, sensory and social potential. Most of the activities were considered either very important or even crucially important. As might be expected for a profoundly disabled person, the progress claimed was modest. The centre claimed progress in feeding while at home it was noted that he had gained the ability to show more concentration and had fewer screaming tantrums.

An Example of a Client Attending the Centre
Based on the Further Education Model
Client A – Male, age-group under 21

Activities	Objectives (as stated by staff)
Social skills*++	Recognise when he needs toilet and indicate this Pattern of toilet training Prepare for future independence
Physiotherapy*++	Maintain extent of physical flexibility
Basic education+	Teach him to concentrate Eye contact To eye point
Home craft+	To extend use of hands To participate as a member of the group
Pottery++	Increase sensory awareness Stimulation
Basic education+	Improving his ability to listen
Craft (puzzles)+	To respond to instructors To concentrate To use materials appropriately
Community project++	Introduce him to new areas, broaden his horizon, show him more of the world To let the world see more of him Language stimulation through surroundings
Social skills++	To make client more socially acceptable Improve self help skills
Social skills, toileting+	More independence
Feeding & toileting++	Enable self help skills to improve To develop independence Social interaction Teach feeding skills Part of programme for development not to be seen as *ordinary* acts for wheelchair people
Feeding++	Self feeding Exercise choice

Activities	Objectives (as stated by staff)
Personal care++	To be able to wash/dry himself To learn parts of his body – awareness of self Increase ability to be able to wash/dry

Physiotherapy++	To improve physical abilities
	To assess and ensure that limbs function,
	  movements are controlled and extended as
	  appropriate
	He appears to enjoy it

Computer	Give him time with the computer
Assessment	Basic education Improve skills
Expressive language – Makaton++	To encourage communication To deal with his stubbornness Teach him to follow commands Recognition of objects
Swimming+	Enjoyment Relaxation Maintaining movement (back-up to physiotherapy)
Music+	Enjoyment Improve sensory skills
Social skills++*	Increase independence Improve skills generally

Key

*   Major activity – at least two full days or equivalent during monitored period

**   Main activity – at least half the time during the monitored period

+   Activity described as *very important* by staff

++   Activity described as *crucially important* by staff

Client B attended the centre closest to the shared living model. Compared with the last case, there was a lack of comprehensiveness in the efforts made to stimulate and develop his potential. He played with puzzles to see if he could 'make different shapes putting pieces in the right places'. More attention might have been given to putting the pieces together in this person's programme. In some respects, for the shared living model, the activities listed do not do justice to what actually happened. Stress was laid on informal interaction between clients and between staff and clients as a whole. For example during meal times this man was deliberately placed in a position where other, more able trainees could see him and talk with him. Also, certainly there were positive outcomes in this case. He was seen as gaining in confidence and it was acknowledged that something had been learnt both at home and at the centre.

At home it was seen that he had learnt something through attending activities for daily living and at the centre his awareness of a sense of time was noted. 'He has learnt quite a lot. He now knows where this centre is'. This comment related to the fact that when the weather was fine he was sometimes pushed in his wheelchair from his home base. He would have indicated that he recognised where the centre was and that he knew something about which way to go. This particular client, however, appeared to be slightly more able than the other examples. Client A, for example, would certainly not be able to play with Lego.

An Example of a Client Attending a Centre Based on the Shared Living Model
Client B – Male, age-group 20–25

Activities	Objectives (as stated by staff)
Activities for daily living+	Basic hygiene Confidence Independence
Puzzles+	To see if he can make different shapes putting pieces in the right places
Sand play+	Getting him to move his hands and arms Good for him
Play musical instruments	Enjoyment
Basic play (Lego)*	Nice to see him building it high
Listening to music**++	None, but staff person commented this was 'the first thing he asks you to do'
Basic conceptual awareness++	To understand groupings To understand what things are used for

Activities	Objectives (as stated by staff)
Craft tiles	To see what he can do,'he puts them all in a straight line'
Drawings with crayons	Not stated
Sanding	(Staff person not interviewed)

Key
* Major activity – at least two full days or equivalent during monitored period
** Main activity – at least half the time during the monitored period
   Activity described as *very important* by staff
++ Activity described as *crucially important* by staff

Client C attended a small centre closest to the social care model and was one of the most disabled people in the whole sample. She was exposed to a quite different set of experiences compared with Client A at the centre closest to the further education model. On the whole she was left to watch others with the exception of efforts to provide physical stimulus and exercise. The home-based assessment clearly stated that nothing was learnt. The centre felt there might have been a slight development in movement as a result of the attention given to her exercises. One felt, however, that this client might have benefited from the intensive and comprehensive programme she might have received had she attended the centre closest to the further education model.

An Example of a Client Attending the Centre Based on the Social Care Education Model
Client C – Female, age-group under 21

Activities	Objectives (as stated by the staff)
Exercise with equipment+	To give her exercise To bring up chest phlegm especially in the winter
Toileting*+	Care
Exercises**+	For her circulation To stop her bending
Physiotherapy (fortnightly)++	For her circulation

Activities	Objectives (as stated by the staff)
Feeding	Care
Listening to music	To see if she can grip
Physiotherapy (fortnightly)++	For her circulation
Feeding	Care
Listening to music	To see of she can grip holding rattle+
Watching bingo+	To mix with others
Being in room with others+	To encourage her to speak To encourage others to speak to her and help her

Key
* Major activity – at least two full days or equivalent during monitored period
** Main activity – at least half the time during the monitored period
+ Activity described as *very important* by staff
++ Activity described as *crucially important* by staff.

These three clients can be regarded as typical of other clients in this group. The contrasting experiences of different centres was also typical. Not represented by the three examples, however, are clients who were treated as a separate group within a special care unit. The centre attended by Client A had a special care unit but the policy, as at some of the other centres, was to integrate clients from the special care unit with others in the centre as much as possible.

Since the late 1980s there have been moves to develop specialist units for people with profound, or profound and multiple, disabilities which are entirely separate from mainstream day centres. Such centres are based on a belief in the possibility of the kind of progress seen in the case of Client A and based on a multi-disciplinary as well as on an educational model.

An early example was the Persondy Centre near Bridgend, South Wales. Another was the Levern Centre in Glasgow, started by ENABLE (then the SSHM) and also the Carrisbrooke Centre at Airdre was another early pioneering Centre near Glasgow, though for clients with severe rather than profound disabilities.

Variations of the small specialist Centre have since included three more in Scotland. The White Top Centre, Dundee, is strictly for clients with profound and multiple disabilities. The Director of the Centre also holds a Chair in Multiple Disabilities at the University of Dundee. The Aveyron Centre, Hamilton, is strictly for clients with a profound mental disability, including some who are able-bodied – although most also have physical and/or sensory handicaps. Finally, the RNIB Springfield Service, Bishopbriggs (Glasgow) is available to people with a severe visual impairment and who also have a learning disability. All three Centres are small and well staffed and provide intensive training which have demonstration and advisory functions for other service providers.

A bold project to include young adults with profound multiple disabilities in a college setting started in 1995 at Telford College, Edinburgh.

Can progress be made with people with profound learning disabilities at your centre? If so, what factors contribute to this and what would further enhance their possibilities for progress?

Inevitably, for people with profound learning disabilities, basic physical care features prominently. In many cases, due to additional physical illness or disabilities, health care issues such as regular medication, toileting, attending to ailments etc. have to occupy a major part of a daily routine. It is essential that there is close collaboration and consistency of care at home and at the centre.

CHAPTER SEVEN

People Who are Elderly

There are probably more elderly people with learning disabilities attending day services than there were when the research was conducted 1985–7. Some are living longer than would have been expected in the past and, amongst these, fewer are resident in hospitals.

There were 11 people in the sample aged over 55 and a further 6 aged between 50 and 54. Approximately two-thirds of both groups were living in hostels or other residential accommodation.

These 17 elderly people were dispersed in 7 out of the 15 centres in the sample. All models of practice, except the recreation and work models, were represented. There was a very wide range of skills and performance. Five clients out of the 17 were at one particular large centre closest to the social care model and all of these were fairly able clients. As with the young, elderly clients were exposed to a wide range of different experiences at centres closest to differing models of practice and the two examples quoted can only illustrate, rather than represent the total spectrum of this variety.

> *Has the more elderly population in your centre changed during the past few years? Are there more less able people who have been discharged from hospitals in the older age-groups?*

Both of the following two examples are based on people aged over 55 who were fairly capable. The first example is from a large centre closest to the social care model.

Client A was physically and mentally fit. He spent at least half his time during the monitored fortnight undertaking contract work. It was stressed that this was not considered to be preparation for future work. An additional major activity was work experience and the specific purpose was said to have been to help him exercise choice and responsibility. This was within an overall policy of preparation for retirement. The thinking behind this was that he would in all probability have to leave the centre and that as he got older it would be policy to enable him to live in the community and this would ultimately mean living by himself. He was in many ways capable of this already and the programme was designed to help him forward to the point where he would be fully capable of living by himself. With the exception of contract work his programme makes some sense in this respect. There might have been other ways of improving time keeping and teaching him to count up to 50. Alternatively if contract work was beneficial as work experience one wonders if this could not have been performed in a normal working environment perhaps through a sheltered placement scheme where he would receive remuneration. The problem would in all probability be his age. The assessment of outcomes suggested that some learning had taken place in relation to domestic activities.

An Example of a Client Attending the Centre
Based on the Social Care Model
Client A – Male, age-group 55–60

Activities	Objectives (as stated by staff)
Contract work**	Helps him to know timekeeping etc. (not preparation for work) Has to count up to 50 when doing corks
Work experience (managing centre tuck shop)*++	Communicating with people. Counting Knowing when supplies run low and choosing fresh supplies (in answer to researcher's question it was explained that this helped client to exercise choice and responsibility within an overall policy of preparation for retirement)
Music, singing+	Stimulant Relaxing

Activities	Objectives (as stated by staff)
Assessment	To find out what we could do for him
Swimming	Possibly to swim without aids More confidence

Key

* Major activity – at least two full days or equivalent during monitored period
** Main activity – at least half the time during the monitored period
+ Activity described as *very important* by staff
++ Activity described as *crucially important* by staff

> *Do elderly people leave your centre on the grounds of retirement? Retirement from what? What alternative services are available when they retire? Have you any information as to whether these services are preferred or what benefits they bring?*

The second example, Client B, was an elderly lady living in a hostel. She attended a small centre following the shared living model. The residential accommodation was on the same site and part of the same administration as the day centre.

Perhaps the most striking feature of the activities in the case of this client is that they might well have been activities pursued in a residential setting, as if there were no day care at all. The question of her age was being approached in an entirely different way from Client A. The overall object appeared to be to sustain her – to 'keep her skills alive'. In spite of this the staff, that is the residential staff, reported an all-round improvement in communication and general confidence. The centre staff acknowledged that nothing had been learnt there except insofar as there had been a general improvement in motivation.

An Example of a Client Attending the Centre Based on the Shared Living Model
Client B – Female, age-group 60–65

Activities	Objectives (as stated by staff)
Laundry hygiene*	Sustain skills Promote self interest Training, hygiene
Domestic	Sense of being useful Keeps her skills alive A sense of responsibility
Sitting by fire chatting **++	To improve depressed frame of mind
Shopping*	Meet needs for cigarettes – enjoys them Outside contacts Meet friends
Complete research diary*	For research purposes Encourage her to be more confident about herself To encourage her to take an interest
Sleeping late	Needs the rest – not very active

Key

*   Major activity – at least two full days or equivalent during monitored period
** Main activity – at least half the time during the monitored period
+   Activity described as *very important* by staff
++ Activity described as *crucially important* by staff

Since the study was carried out, elderly people have come to form a higher proportion of the general population. Many people with learning disabilities are living longer than could have been expected previously. Attention has been focused on developing services for elderly people, but not enough attention has been paid to the particular needs of elderly people with learning disabilities.

For example, the problems of supporting people with dementia and their carers has emerged as a major social policy issue. Research has shown not only that people with learning disabilities, along with others, are tending to live longer, and are as prone as others to suffer from dementia, but that people with Downs Syndrome are very likely to begin to show symptoms of Alzheimer's disease; although the time when this happens will vary from early fifties to late sixties. Many other people with learning disabilities will increasingly suffer from multiple disabilities including sensory impairments as they become older. On the other hand, some elderly people with learning disabilities, like Case A will remain physically fit and active. I recently studied a person in their late seventies, living in a hostel, who had to be advised to discontinue cycling!

It is not clear that there is a policy for day services for elderly people with learning disabilities. Individual arrangements for particular clients should be in the context of care management plans which take into account services as a whole for elderly people and their carers. Carers will certainly value day services as respite. Clients will also often value a break from home carers. Residential respite will also enhance the quality of living for carers and help in a transition, where necessary, to residential care in the case of some elderly people with learning disabilities who also suffer from dementia. (For a detailed recent study of these issues, as affecting elderly people in general, see Levin *et al. Better for the Break*, National Institute for Social Work Research Unit, HMSO 1994).

> *Does your centre have a policy with regard to elderly people? Does this include a policy with regard to people showing symptoms of dementia?*

CHAPTER EIGHT

Moving On?

Research in the early 1980s had established that the annual percentage of clients who moved on from day centres was very small. The findings of our research in 1985–7 suggested that it was slightly increasing at that time – it also showed that the proportion varied substantially between one model of practice and another.

Out of the sample of 146 clients, 15 (10%) had ceased to attend centres during the twelve months preceding the end of the research period. From the larger total number of all the 808 clients in the 15 selected centres, 75 (9%) had left during the same period.

The figure below shows how the proportion of the 75 who had left varied between the seven models of centre practice.

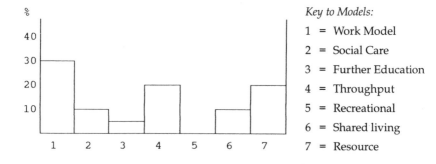

The percentage throughput during the twelve-month period varied from 0 per cent in the case of the recreational model (one centre) to 29 per cent in the case of the work model (one centre). For the two largest groups of centres, namely those closest to the social care model (5 centres) and the further education model (3 centres) the percentage throughput was 7 per cent and 6 per cent respectively. However, one of the centres in the further education group was only opened at the beginning of the research period and it would perhaps be unreasonable to expect a typical throughput during its first year of operation. If this centre is excluded, the percentage throughput for centres closest to the further education model would be 7 per cent. It should also be borne in mind that in one of the social care centres the throughput was nil and in another centre the throughput was 16 per cent.

Throughput was not necessarily a stated objective for all models. This applied to the recreational and the shared living models although it might happen as a by-product of a client's greater potential being realised.

Statistics in themselves are of limited use. Their reliability was dubious because centres applied different rules about what constituted leaving. For example, one of the centres only took clients initially for a limited period which was less than one year. By one criterion, therefore, its throughput could be defined as 100 per cent. However, when the courses were ended clients might continue to be supported on a part-time basis, and, for this purpose they continued on the register. This centre only counted clients as leaving who were no longer on the register. Other centres kept some clients on their registers for some time after they had left, in case they might return.

The validity of the idea of throughput was questionable because, for example, deaths and families who had moved out of the area or clients who had moved to other centres for administrative reasons, were included as well as others who had made a positive move, say to obtain employment.

Qualitative data on these possibilities from the total number of clients attending the 15 centres were limited, but some significant positive moves were noted. For example, in the case of the work centre, a total of 13 clients were recorded as having left. Of these, five went into open or sheltered employment and five left for work experience. One left to attend another day centre, one left for domestic reasons and one died. (Those who left for work experience remained on the register.) This appeared to be the most impressive case of positive throughput on the basis of the data given.

In the case of the two centres closest to the assessment and throughput model (taken together), a total of 18 clients left. Four of these obtained open or sheltered employment, four obtained work experience, four went to further education colleges, two to other day care centres, two returned to be unemployed at home and two left because of particular domestic circumstances. The most negative findings for positive throughput, as distinct from throughput in general, were perhaps those recorded for the social care model centres. No-one from these centres left for open or sheltered work, or for work experience.

How many people move on from your centre, on average, in a year? Where do they go to? How do the figures compare with those given above?

Where no employment or further training opportunities were found, leaving a centre might be seen as a move from *pretend work* to being officially unemployed. This raises important issues as the following three examples show.

Example 1 – Jim, age-group 45–50

Jim lived in a hostel and used to attend a centre which was closest to the social care model. He had attended and lived in the hostel for a long time. Progress had been recorded both by centre and by hostel staff mostly in domestic activities and, in particular in cooking for himself. At the hostel there was a plan worked out with Jim that he should move to a flat. Trial periods in lodgings occurred during the research, but at the conclusion of the research period he was in a bed-sit within the hostel. He was unemployed.

Social networks before and after Jim left the Centre were compared. The extent of his visiting from home increased from 6 to 9 visits during fortnightly periods. The types of contacts did not substantially change. Both networks showed a number of solo activities and these increased during the second fortnight. The bulk of his visits were for shopping and other daily living tasks. During the first period he attended a club. During the second period, while on holiday, he visited a pub. He does not seem to have had many friends. Two relatives and a residential care worker were identified as his 'important people'. Their main benefit to him was their feelings of affection. The care worker was identified by Jim as helpful because she had tried to find placements with landladies.

What conclusions can we draw ? First, it did not appear that the centre was indispensable for Jim's progress towards independent living or for his learning new things. The thrust of training for independent living came from the hostel staff rather than from the centre staff.

Second, activities important to him at home included more personal attention to himself such as baths, washing hair and putting on lotion etc. He seemed to be gaining in self-esteem. This could be because he had moved to a bed-sit, though still within the hostel. It could be because of the efforts of hostel staff. It could also be partly because he had left the centre and developed a pattern of living which was apart from other disabled people.

It appeared, therefore, that throughput from the centre was positive. The main credit for this should go, if to anybody besides Jim himself (for he set the pace in demanding his own leaving), to the hostel staff rather than to the centre staff. However, it should be remembered that the centre probably contributed to Jim's learning at an earlier stage.

Jim still had a long way to go and the networks illustrated the extent of his need for an enriched social life outside group activities within, or emanating from, the hostel before he could be expected to settle perhaps with a landlady or in a flat.

Example 2 – Alan, age-group 35–40

Alan lived in a flat with his brother. Their parents had died fifteen years earlier but he was in contact with other members of the family.

Alan had a physical handicap while his learning disability would be regarded as mild. He could perform all self-management and daily living tasks listed in the research schedule. He was also reasonably literate. He kept his own diary during the first monitored fortnight of research with a minimum of support from his brother.

The centre Alan had attended was closest to the resource centre model, with part-time attendance being regarded as normal. At the start of the first monitored fortnight, he was suspended from regular attendance. His behaviour had been described as disruptive. Nevertheless he visited the centre unofficially four times.

Between monitored periods, regular part-time attendance was resumed. However, by the time of the final monitored fortnight, he had decided to leave, with the arrangement that he came still on the days set aside for what was called a *drop-in club*, when he would have the opportunity to discuss his problems (now that he had left) with the manager. In other words, this particular centre expected to be able to offer continued support to trainees who had officially left.

Alan was well able to express his mixed feelings about the centre. He told the researcher: 'I've enjoyed my years at the centre. I've made a lot of good friends there, people I would not have known otherwise.' Yet on an earlier occasion he had said it was '50% good and 50% bad':

> It's sometimes like being back at school. We're supposed to be grown up. But we are treated as though we were at school. Ah well, that's the rules – I try and break them.

Alan had previously attended a more conventional Centre full-time. But he had been suspended for walking out (and going to the pub) and that was how he came to be referred to the Centre where part-time attendance was recognised. Other details of his past were not revealed, but he did say he wished he had been able to go to a full-time centre when he was much younger. He felt he had missed out.

> I realise now that I should have been in a centre years ago. I might have been pushed more, less dependent on my mother.

The social network for the second monitored period showed that Alan's pattern of life, revolving around daytime *survival* activities and evening visits to the pub had not changed. Friends at the pub were only referred to vaguely and were not described as important. There had been deeper involvement with people at the centre. Again, he mad mixed feelings about this.

> You become very attached to different people through the Centre. This is not always a good thing – the emotional problems.

The research gave a detailed picture of some of his close relationships with other trainees over a period of time. The staff were aware of his need for a stable and intimate relationship, but was the centre the best environment (any more than, perhaps, the pub) for him to expect to find it? A relationship with a much younger trainee had floundered when she did not welcome his advances. A relationship which the staff regarded as more helpful was with a trainee who was more physically handicapped and who gave an opportunity to Alan to be helpful, without feeling he was being pushed to help.

After Alan had left the centre, the only important relationship outside home was with his sister. She was a means of access to other members of the family. She helped him, for example, with washing and money. She offered affection and he was also able to do things for her.

It seems that Alan, not uncommonly amongst people with mild learning disabilities living in the community, needed assistance in developing a helpful social network. This case exposed the question of who should be the person to offer this help. Does it fall between the centre and other social services? A social worker was recorded as visiting during the first monitored fortnight. The reason for the visit could not be explained by the recipient. It was not even clear whether it was to do with Alan or his brother. It was not, apparently, either very meaningful or helpful. Here again, as with the first case studied (Jim), throughput to the status of being unemployed at home did not have a neat positive or negative connotation. What could be said was that it raised further questions about follow-up after clients had left. The resource centre model of practice had the potential advantages that follow-up was built into the expected practice. But this still does not answer the question *Who has the prime responsibility for support?* or, more particularly, *Who should help the client develop the means of support from within a helping network which can include formal and informal sources of help?*

What issues does this case raise for care management? Suggest the main ingredients of a possible care package.

Example 3 – Marion, age-group 30–35

Marion lived in a group home. She was regularly supported by a social worker. She had twice been in open employment before attending a centre. She said she had given up employment to help look after other members of the family. It was also claimed, and confirmed by the social worker, that other members of the family took advantage of her and borrowed money from her when she could not easily reckon it up, for example. Understanding money was the one complex task she could not manage without assistance.

During the first monitoring period, Marion told the researcher she was fed up 'with them at the ATC' and wanted to stay at home. Her activities were somewhat restricted at the centre but the staff were supportive in allowing her to go out from the centre or to take time off to claim benefit.

Amongst the points that could be noted from her social network were the following: first, it was a rich network with friends, neighbours and relations all involved. People visited her at home. She visited others and had a wide range of activities. Second, Marion was capable of walking and using public transport, but nevertheless relied on the centre minibus for visits out from the centre. She also used it to get to the centre, although sometimes she walked. Third, the centre did not appear to be contributing qualitatively to her network. Centre activities replicated the kinds of things she could already do at home. An expedition from the centre to the shopping centre might have been one occasion to help her to learn to use money. The centre was not doing anything else specifically, let alone intensively, to help her in this.

Marion's life changed. She decided to leave the centre and was supported by the social worker in doing so. Then she became engaged to Jack. She left the group home and married. During this time she received considerable support from the social worker.

The centre was a large one, closest to the social care model. At its best, this model would suggest that the centre could serve as back-up to the individualised attention co-ordinated and primarily provided by the social worker. When Marion was anxious to find a job, the centre supported her in making job applications and helping her to fill out the necessary forms. She was not successful in finding work. In spite of this, being unemployed at home cannot be said to have been a failure. The outcome of attendance at the centre, together with the outcome of the support given by the social worker was satisfactory in most respects.

Some general points emerge from these three examples of throughput from centres where the outcome was unemployed at home. First, it will be noted that the three clients were all relatively able people with only mild learning disabilities.

Second, the initiative for leaving came from the clients themselves in all three cases. Once they had decided to leave, they each received support in varying ways. Jim was supported by the residential hostel staff, Alan by the centre manager and Marion by the field social worker.

Finally, we can see that being unemployed at home meant different things for each of the three clients in terms of the richness of their social lives and activities. Jim still lived largely in the world of learning disability, although his ambition was to find a flat of his own. He needed preparation for this. Alan had a flat of his own (or, at least, one he shared with his brother). His social life, however, could be described mainly as survival living. He had needs to develop relationships with other people which were not being fulfilled, except for the relationship with his sister. Marion, on the other hand, who already lived in a group home had developed a full and normal life outside the centre even while she was attending it. It can be said that she ceased to attend when the centre became superfluous to her needs.

The question may be asked, whether these three people should have gone to day centres in the first place. In Jim's case with the support he had at the hostel, one might question whether full-time attendance at a centre for other people with learning disabilities was holding him back from developing his self-esteem in more normal settings. Alan was clear that he had needed to attend a centre and he wished he had been able to do so earlier on his life. He felt, however, that he out-grew it when he reached an age when he wanted to be more independent. Marion appeared to have needed support at an earlier stage when she was working. Intensive support by a social worker might have provided alternatives to centre attendance at that time. On the other hand the flexibility and the individualisation provided at the centre in keeping with the social care model worked in her case – in spite of the centre size. She was neither lacking in self-esteem (as Jim was) nor rebellious (like Alan). She tended to fit in and one wonders, had she not herself wished to leave, whether or not the centre would have come to appreciate that her needs could be met elsewhere? Where would Marion have been without the support of the social worker in wanting to leave the centre?

Other examples of positive throughput, to obtain work or to attend an FE college for example, were associated with the assessment and throughput model. One client who obtained open employment illustrates what can be done. This particular person had come from a long stay mental hospital, through an intermediate residential establishment, to share the tenancy of a council house. The centre specifically promoted these moves, through a phased and committed programme, to cope with both work and living independently. He remained in stable employment for many years and the centre and other agencies continued to support him.

Clients' Views

We asked clients 'Have you ever thought you would like to do something else/go somewhere else other than to this centre?' Out of a total of 93 who gave answers, 57 (61%) said they would like to do something else or go somewhere else. Thirty-six (39%) said they would prefer to stay at the centre where they were. Of those who wanted to move the following were the preferences given:

Paid work	19
Further Education College	18
Stay at home	8
Another Adult Training Centre	4
Unpaid work experience	2
Other answers	6
Total	**57**

With only about 10 per cent annual throughput and only a proportion of this positive throughput, it was an important finding that as many as 61 per cent of clients were wanting to move. These are some of the comments of those who wanted to move:

- I want a job. It doesn't matter about the money.

  In the case below, the client specifically asked the researcher to write the answer down:

- Write down I want a job – a real job – I will be 24 soon. I need a job, any job.

- I'd like to go to college, but who would take me home?

- College maybe. Already I do quite a lot voluntarily in the evenings. I wouldn't rather have a job.

- I would like to work somewhere else. I'm fed-up with the Centre.

- I would like to help the old people two mornings a week – if paid, my allowances would be affected.

Examples show that all of these kinds of aspirations can be met and sometimes are met today. But does this happen in all instances?

These are some of the comments of those who wanted to stay at their Centre:

- I'd like to stay here – I like it here.

- Until the new (Centre) opens, it's better here than walking the streets in the bad weather.

- I would like to keep it just three days a week – I prefer my clubs. *(A client attending part-time.)*

- I would like to stay here because of my girlfriend.

Some clients felt that they wanted to leave the centre and go to work but that they could not do so because of physical disability. For example one client said 'I cannot work because I am unable to lift anything heavy'.

If the rate of positive throughput was increasing, the evidence from clients suggested it would have to accelerate a lot more before it met their expressed wishes for the future.

> *If people at your centre were asked if they would like to be doing something else, what kinds of answers would you expect?*

CHAPTER NINE

Moves to More Independent Living

All seven models of practice subscribed to the aim of promoting more independent living. During the course of the research, ten people (7% of the total sample) moved to more independent forms of living. Of these:

- 1 moved from a large residential institution to a hostel
- 3 moved from hostels to sheltered flats or other sheltered accommodation
- 1 moved from a hostel to an ordinary tenancy
- 1 moved from parents to a hostel
- 1 moved from parents to lodging house
- 2 moved from parents to lodgings
- 1 moved from a group home to an ordinary tenancy

One would expect there to be relatively more people attending centres today who have left long-stay hospitals. Has there also been any increase in the numbers leaving the parental home at an earlier age than in the past, in order to live independently away from parents?

Seven of the above represented moves to situations where, for the first time, clients were responsible for paying their own rent. During the research period the number of day-service-users responsible for paying their rent doubled.

All those who moved could be described as having a mild or moderate learning disability. With one exception (the person who moved from a large institution) they were all aged under 37. Two were aged under 20.

The two following examples illustrate the kinds of circumstances in which clients moved to more independent forms of living and the part played by centres.

Most centre models of practice incorporated some kind of activities aimed at training for more independent daily living. *Survival skills* was (and is) one popular term for this. In the majority of cases these activities had not led, during the research period at least, to moves to more independent living. Moreover in one of the cases illustrated (Andrew), where a move did take place, such activities were considered less important than other activities. Domestic activities did feature in Angela's case, but in the same way, learning at the hostel was seen as more significant.

Example 1 – Andrew, age-group 30–35

This is an example of a move away from parents in strained circumstances.

Although there are cultural and class differences affecting the age when the majority of people in the population as a whole move away from parents, most people with disabilities stay at home much longer than their brothers or sisters do. Our research came across a considerable number of cases where clients living with parents wanted to leave. It seemed to us that in some cases behaviour described as challenging, reflected the client's wish for greater independence, often occurring when clients were in their late twenties or thirties.

Do you know of cases of challenging behaviour where wanting to leave home could be part of the picture? How would you set about planning with the client and carers to achieve this?

This was true for Andrew. His need to leave home, and the problems the parents had with him, were recognised at the centre and he was not just treated as having a behaviour problem.

Andrew lived a restricted life at home during the first monitored fortnight. His centre, closest to the resource centre model, was based on part-time attendance. It was assumed that the centre staff, and particularly the manager, had a part to play in the home life of clients like Andrew outside the centre. Thus the manager (who was a qualified social worker) visited Andrew at home and Andrew attended the centre twice.

The manager was trying to understand and to help the parents with their own situation. In the event, circumstances precipitated Andrew's departure from home. After an incident at the centre involving drinking and violence the police were called in. The resulting charge led to Andrew spending a period in prison. On his release, the parents refused to have him back in the house and the only place he could find to stay was at a lodging house. At this point the centre tried to refer Andrew to a specialist social work team concerned with homeless persons but they refused to take him because they considered he was inappropriately placed in the lodging house and that, therefore, he was outside their remit.

After a while, Andrew settled down. During a second monitored fortnight, his pattern of his life was studied after the move to the lodging house. He visited his mum and dad every other day. His drinking was less prominent and he was engaged in a wider range of visits, for example he had to go shopping before he could cook a meal. Meanwhile other contacts such as a visit to a home for the elderly to play bowls with residents were encouraged by the centre and on one occasion, the deputy manager accompanied him on a visit to his parents.

While previously Andrew had been disruptive (at the centre as well as at home) he now stressed to the researcher that he did not want to put his place at the centre 'at risk again'.

The lodging house move was regarded by Andrew as temporary. His ambition was a flat and he was working with the centre in preparing for this at the time the research ended. He commented: 'I am going to start cooking...the centre manager said I might be getting a flat soon'.

The role of the centre in this case was not so much in terms of educational activities, at least during the research period, as in providing a supportive social environment. The centre became very important in Andrew's life, but not in terms of aims tradition-ally associated with ATCs, such as social education. Rather the centre provided stability, reality, friendship and acceptance in Andrew's life. Andrew himself said that he found it a lot easier to talk and mix with people in the centre than he would outside. Within the centre the social interactions were more clearly defined for Andrew than they would be outside where he might be meeting people on his own without the support of others.

The principles of community care should make it easier to deal with people as individuals who cross over categories such as the homeless, ex-offenders or those with learning disabilities. Would the new approach have helped Andrew?

Example 2 – Angela, age-group under 21

This is an example of a move from a hostel to more independent living in a staffed house.

At the time the research started, Angela had come to live in a hostel, with sixteen other residents, after her mother had re-married. She required no more than minimum support to perform both self-management and daily living skills. During the course of the research she moved to a smaller community house run by a voluntary organisation.

During the first monitored fortnight she had a lot of activities out from the centre including visits for shopping on the way back to the hostel. It was a long journey to the hostel involving a change of buses.

There was a second monitored fortnight after the move had taken place. She now stayed overnight with her boyfriend, whom she planned to marry. She was leading a busy life, largely centred on her fiancé on the one hand, and the other residents at the house on the other.

The staff at the centre noted a change in her behaviour after the move. 'There is a big improvement since she settled', one staff member said. Another staff member explained that they were careful not to overload Angela with domestic activities. She needed 'a little domestic help – not a lot, but enough to encourage her to be more ordered.'

In general, the centre did not claim particular credit for the move but staff stated that improvements and learning had taken place as a result. The key worker at the centre noted that her hygiene had improved but this was not attributed directly to work at the centre. The centre activities which Angela herself said she liked after the move were woodwork and art as well as sewing and domestic.

The centre, however, was actively aware of what was going on in the community house. The key worker at the centre met community house staff and the latter were shown round the centre.

The centre in this case was closest to the further education model.

What does Angela's case tell us about collaboration between hostel and centre staff in preparing for moving to more independent living?

CHAPTER TEN

Do Centres Support Clients Living Independently?

'No man is an island'. We use the word 'independently' with this reservation. The paradox of promoting independence is that it consists in enabling clients to be interdependent in their relationships with others in order minimally to survive but, more ambitiously, to lead richer, more mature and fulfilling lives outside their parents' homes and outside residential institutions.

Fourteen clients were living independently throughout the research period in the minimal sense of living away from their parents and being responsible for their own rent. They were attending centres closest to particular models of practice as follows:

Resource Centre Model (from the same centre)	5
Social Care Model (3 from the same centre, 1 from another centre)	4
Further Education Model (each of the 3 centres closest to this model being included)	4
Work Model	1

Example 1 – Iain, age-group 45–50

Iain, who suffers from arthritis, lived in a top floor council flat in a three-storey block. It was situated in a run-down council estate, with intersecting busy main roads nearby. There were shops opposite and a shopping centre ten minutes' walk away – but the nearest phone box was further away.

Iain lived by himself. After his parents had died, some twenty years earlier, he had lived in 'a lovely home I shared with my sister'. But his sister went into hospital and then in his own words:

> I smashed up the house. I was drinking heavily. For the next 14 years my sister was in hospital and I continued to drink. I stayed in various lodging houses and skippered. Then one day I decided I had to pull myself together and now I rarely take a drink.

It was not clear how he was then offered the tenancy of a flat. He said 'when they were doing up my flat a social worker asked me to go to the centre. I thought it was alright'. He had, in fact, been helping in an old people's club which shared the same building with the adult training centre. He would, therefore, have known about the centre. He was registered at the centre two days a week a few months before the research started.

During the first monitored fortnight his sister was his only visitor. He went for walks by himself to shop, pay the rent, and to attend a church club for homeless men. His role there was now as a helper. He also walked his dog. On one occasion he took a train into the city centre to go to the pictures, but again he went by himself. At home he described his activities as sitting around, making tea for his sister, watching TV or radio, playing snooker or tidying up. At the centre (which was only a few minutes' walk away) he was involved in domestic duties, craft work, and a variety of other activities.

During an update visit, the researcher reported that an instructor at the centre was helping Iain at home after he had transferred to another council flat in the same area. He was being assisted in a housing grant application, shopping for his house and arranging redecoration. His attendance at the centre increased from two to three days a week.

The second monitoring period, nine months later, showed Iain's now much more extensive social network. He had made contact with a sister and cousin who were temporarily staying with him. His visitors included a particular friend, Morag. Through the centre he had begun attending a college course which included basic education. His centre activities were more specifically directed to his needs at home. His own efforts to reconstruct his life appeared to be supported.

In answer to questions about what he had learnt at the centre he replied:

> How to fill in forms better. Cooking perhaps. Reading and writing, going to college.

The staff assessment was that he was walking better without his stick and was not as quiet as he had been – he had learnt to back-chat. In a summary reviewing Iain's progress, the researcher wrote:

> Despite his somewhat unkempt appearance (the many layers of clothing necessary to the long-term homeless) he has an air of dignity, as he gives his definite views on how to deal with housing officials, DHSS etc. I feel the centre is probably offering him the ability to muddle more effectively through the demands that living on his own places on him.

The researcher then listed specific areas where help had been given including dealing with past debts and applying for the housing grant to improve his home surroundings. The researcher continued:

> The recreational aspect of having somewhere to attend each day is probably important as well, though it is fair to say that Iain's life would not be totally isolated without the centre, because of his contacts with the other club he attends for the homeless. He has problems with budgeting still. The way the centre helps probably reflects a social work office, or welfare rights office rather than the traditional adult training centre. The key worker is involved directly with Iain, helping him to spend his housing grant sensibly and monitoring the payment of bills as they arrive. Iain also benefits from the informal discussion groups at the centre. While he tends to be an advisor in such groups, pointing out to other clients how to deal with awkward neighbours etc., my impressions are that he would quietly take in what others were saying and perhaps adapt his own methods accordingly.

Iain himself saw the centre in very positive terms. Except for one client, he said, others at the centre and the staff were friendly. He particularly enjoyed craft work, cooking, football and jogging, swimming and discussions. When he was asked whether he would ever like to do something else rather than attend the present centre he said 'No, he would like to stay there'.

In the follow-up, after the second monitored fortnight, three important places for Iain were the homeless club, where he helped; the cinema, which he enjoyed occasionally; and Mass where he went every Sunday. Two important people were named, his sister and his friend Morag. Of his sister he said 'She's the only one (relation) I've got. We help each other'. It was his sister who had introduced him to Morag. His sister also helped Iain make dinners and, in return, he said 'I advise her and keep her right. I've got to, she's my responsibility'. Asked whether he had a particular member of staff who was important to him he named a person and added 'because she is my key worker'. There was no particular client at the centre he wanted to nominate as being helpful to him.

What factors contributed to the progress made in this case? Are this kind of support and outcome common today? (This was a fairly exceptional case in 1987).

Example 2 – Gordon, age-group 35–40

Gordon lived in a modern council house in what the researcher described as a very nice estate in a town. The access to facilities was relatively good, with a bus five minutes' walk away. He took over the tenancy of the house from his father who, at the beginning of the research, was in hospital and shortly afterwards died. Gordon's sister and brother-in-law offered to accommodate him but he preferred to stay on his own. Nevertheless he depended on them for help.

During the first monitored fortnight his sister visited daily to wake him up. His brother visited to light the fire. Other relations were also in close touch. Gordon travelled by bus for a variety of purposes and by train and bus to visit his girlfriend at a hostel. He had inherited a rich network of contacts from his family but this was supplemented by his own interests, including boxing. He attended night school 'to learn to read and write'. His activities at home included homework for this. Otherwise at home his activities suggested he was mainly concerned with keeping house and watching television and radio. However, he spent much of his time away from his house.

At the centre Gordon was mainly involved in work activities but also some reading, singing and listening to the radio. He had attended this centre since it opened. The centre, closest to the work centre model did not usually seek to be involved in client's home situations. In this case, however, a further factor concerning Gordon was that he was epileptic and it is recorded, during the update between the two monitoring fortnights that the centre manager had phoned the sister-in-law several times when Gordon had suffered fits to ask what to do. The sister told the researcher she had mentioned Gordon's loneliness. There had also been some unofficial contact between one of the instructors and the family. But, by this time, Gordon was receiving the help he needed in managing at home from his relations and not from the centre. Gordon said 'My sister still gets me up and my brother lights the fire'. He also said, because of the time spent in visiting his father in hospital, he had given up his boxing.

This centre would not claim to have helped him at home and nor did Gordon, or his relations expect this. It was looked upon as a work centre and the regret of the relatives was that it had not been more successful in finding him employment. The instructor working with Gordon regretted this too and said 'There should be a sheltered workshop with trained personnel in the work tasks involved'.

During the second monitored fortnight (nine months later), five days were spent at a respite holiday home. He also had an overnight stay with one of his sisters.

The main event for Gordon between the two monitored periods was the death of his father in hospital. This was described as something of a release because, although he could not help his father, he had spent time visiting him and it had in some ways restricted his life. In the second monitored fortnight there was an increase in activity. This was mainly within the extended family who offered hospitality. Gordon's boxing was resumed and he also attended a rugby game and a boxing competition.

During both monitored fortnights Gordon had contact with a social worker. During the first fortnight the social worker visited him and during the second fortnight he visited the Social Work Department from the centre. Gordon said the social worker had helped him to fill in a job application form for a gardener's assistant. He was not assessed as having made any progress or learnt anything during the year under review as a result of attending the centre either by his sister or by the centre staff.

Gordon identified the respite holiday home, boxing, and his relations' houses as his important places. The important people were all relations. One sister 'helps me a lot'. A nephew taught him boxing. In particular his sister 'helps me by making my breakfast every morning, round the house, and I go for dinner.' She had also provided access to other members of her family. There were very similar comments concerning his sister-in-law. His nephew had been helpful in gaining access to others at boxing and with training. All three relations offered affection. There was no mention of important people being helpful at the centre, either staff or other clients. In summarising Gordon's situation, the researcher wrote:

> My impressions were that his sister-in-law and brother, who are regarded as the main support people, have a very caring, although not overprotective attitude towards Gordon.

Comparing these two examples we can see that Iain had a very restricted natural helping network. Gordon had a rich network of relations, and through relations, friends. The death of Iain's parents had occurred a long time previously and he went through a period of intense loneliness and homelessness before being able to restructure and reconstruct his life through the support he found at first in the church and latterly also through the centre he came to attend on a part-time basis.

Gordon's father had died only recently and in his particular circumstances it was seen as a release, an event which was enabling to him rather than disabling. The centre that Gordon attended, although full-time, had a much more restricted role. It was oriented to work experience and occupation in the absence of success in finding outside employment – although attempts were still being made to find employment.

The centre offered exactly what Iain needed at the right time. Yet he had only recently started to attend. Other facets of his life had taken prominence over any definition of *learning disability*. He was first and foremost homeless. This overlaid, or took precedence over, the emergence of mental disability as an issue and thereby denied

him access to a day centre which was intended for people with
learning disabilities.

Gordon's centre in contrast was a work centre. It was only
peripherally (and in this case on medical grounds) concerned with
his home life. Here the question must be raised of where Gordon
would have been without the support from his family. He could
very easily have become homeless, as Iain had been, 20 years
earlier.

*These examples illustrate the importance of informal helping
networks in sustaining maximum independence in the community. Are such networks studied and understood in planning
activities at centres as well as in formulating community care
plans?*

CHAPTER 11

Do Centres Promote Integration with the Community?

All seven models of practice claimed to be associated with promoting integration. This took various forms. It was intended, for example, that integration should be achieved through work in the case of the work model or through mixing in the community in the case of the social care model. The further education model stressed education as helping clients become more integrated within the community, by learning to use educational, leisure, and other 'normal' services and facilities. The recreational model hoped to promote contacts through sporting activities and using sports facilities. The shared living model possibly represented a tendency for clients to be encapsulated within centres, but it was also argued that shared living aimed to give clients confidence in learning to reach out to others.

The throughput and resource centre models were most explicitly related to integration with the community. Positive throughput meant promoting integration whether it was throughput to work experience, voluntary or paid employment, further education or occupation outside the centre. The resource centre model saw the centre as a resource for clients, their families and the wider community including those who were helping to facilitate people with learning disabilities in living more normal lives.

How much of all this was just rhetoric? During the 1985–87 study we looked closely at whether in practice clients mixed with non-disabled people as a direct consequence of attending centres. During the first monitored fortnight only 14 clients (10%) out of the 139 for whom information was obtained, made visits outside their centres in company with groups of other clients, which involved mixing mainly with non-disabled people. A further 28 (20%) of the sample of 139 went out from the centre on their own. It may be assumed that most of these visits would have entailed some contact with other non-disabled people in the community.

The incidence of clients mixing mainly with other *non-disabled* people in the community came from centres closest to the following models of practice:

Model	Clients visiting		
	In groups	*On their own*	*Total*
Work	0	2	2
Social Care	5	7	12
Further Education	2	5	7
Throughput	3	5	8
Recreational	0	1	1
Shared Living	1	5	6
Resource Centre	7	5	12
Total	**18**	**30**	**48**

These figures did not take account of part-time attenders many of whom spent whole days away from the centre mixing with others at colleges or undertaking work experience, for example.

Bearing in mind that there were many more clients attending centres closest to the Social Care Model than centres closest to other models, the figures show that there was very small chance indeed of clients mixing with non-disabled people in the community. Clients attending the Resource Centre Model had the best chance of so doing. The resource centre also had by far the largest proportion of part-time attenders who would be more likely to mix with non-disabled people on non-attendance days.

There was a much higher frequency of group visits from centres into the community which involved mixing mainly with other disabled people. In fact of the 139 clients for whom data was available during the first monitored fortnight only ten were not involved in group visits of this kind. In slightly more than half the cases, such visits were on average daily occurrences.

What chance do users of your day service have of mixing with non-disabled people while they are attending? Have the chances increased during the past year?

Day-service users were, and probably still are, more likely to mix with non-disabled people during the time they were at home than while they were attending day centres.

The frequency of clients mixing in groups with other non-disabled people, or going on visits by themselves, was greater for home-based networks than for centre-based networks. Of 141 clients for whom data was available on home-based networks during the first monitored fortnight, 103 (73%) were involved in visits with one or two others which mainly involved mixing with non-disabled people. Sixty-four (45%) made visits from home by themselves during the same fortnight. The percentage figures for the second monitored fortnight were similar.

There was no evidence, therefore, that centres *per se* contributed to the process of enabling individual clients to mix with non-disabled people in the large majority of cases. It might even have been the reverse. By attending centres and going out only with other people with learning disabilities, the clients were actually restricted in their opportunities for mixing with more non-disabled people.

Indeed attendance at some centres promoted greater involvement in the world of learning disability even at home in that special clubs for others with mental handicap, directly or indirectly associated with centre activities, are encouraged; for example, by the use of centre transport.

There were, however, a small minority – the exceptions – where attendance at the centre was closely linked with facilitating involvement with more normal activities outside. These were centres where integration was a very specific, and not simply a general aim and where specific activities were directed towards its achievement.

For instance one of the two centres closest to the throughput model was specifically concerned with *outreach* into the local community. The project itself was situated in a larger building where a number of other community projects were housed. Opportunities for integration, therefore, existed within the building itself. The number of clients involved in the outreach project was very small compared with the numbers of other people in the building. The clients, called *workers* were only on their own, in group discussions or meetings, for the minimum of time. They met, for example, to plan their week on an individualised basis depending on their objectives during their fixed period of attendance. All of them were involved in some kind of experience which might begin within the building helping with other activities for other client groups (for example groups of elderly people) or outside the centre altogether in other projects. Therefore, mixing with normal people was at a far higher level than was normally the case at other centres. (It was because the numbers were so small at this centre and our sample accordingly small, that this does not show up fully in the statistics at the beginning of this chapter).

Some centres in the sample encouraged visitors. One of the centres closest to the throughput model opened a cafe on centre premises where a group of trainees was involved in preparing snacks and serving customers. However, it was not particularly well patronised and there was not enough to do. A normal cafe premises would have been a more effective venue and in this case the idea would have been transformed into a kind of co-operative form of work, or work experience. Few centres are situated in an ideal place where the general public can just conveniently drop in.

Perhaps your centre has some facility open to the general public. If so, how far are the kinds of problems mentioned above familiar to you? How are they overcome?

What other schemes do you have specifically aimed at promoting significant contacts with non-disabled people?

Centres closest to the Shared Living Model, while in some ways tending to be a world of their own, can counter this tendency in terms of inviting the outside world to come to them. One of the centres closest to this model was moving in this direction by turning craft work, traditionally seen as occupation, into an ex-panding industry with a turnover large enough to be registered for

VAT purposes. Clients and staff put considerable effort into this business. Because it was craft work there was a lot of emphasis both on job satisfaction and creating something saleable. However, only a few clients were involved directly in the sales and therefore this centre's approach was not at that time particularly geared to integration with the local community – although it might be seen to have other benefits. It could have been developed further if more clients had helped in running the shop and also developing the business in other ways which involved outreach into the community.

This aspect of integration has certainly developed in recent years. One centre in the South-East of England for example runs a successful catering business delivering high quality meals to groups. Other centres are developing other kinds of small business enterprises. This aspect of the enterprise culture may have promoted more contacts between people attending day centres and the general public. How far this leads to relationships and not just contacts is another question.

The extent to which centres promote integration with the community – a key issue in terms of aims – appeared from our research to be hindered because of counter tendencies and influences towards segregation. The general answer to the question 'Do clients mix with non-disabled people as a consequence of attending centres?' was in the large majority of cases at that time, 'no'. This was because the general orientation of centres, whatever their stated aims, was to provide activities within a fairly closed or segregated social environment. This environment provided stability and offered many social assets within its own confines. Efforts to break out tended to have a token significance because clients were usually in groups. The extent of their integration, in most cases, tended to be symbolic. The majority had far more integration within the community from their home-base.

> *Do clients mix with normal people more as a result of attendance at your centre? There may be very different answers for different people attending.*

CHAPTER TWELVE

Does Attendance at a Centre Enhance the Quality of Life at Home?

Integration is not necessarily an end in itself or even the most important objective for all day service attenders. A broader goal is to enhance the client's quality of life at home – wherever home is. Patterns of living at home were studied by means of social network analysis. The data was gathered from daily diaries kept during two monitored fortnights with follow-up discussions about significant people and places plus researchers' assessments (from the research data as a whole). Networks at home were classified as *self-contained* (inward looking) or *embracing* (outward looking with a rich variety of contacts). Parents' attitudes were also classified in terms of whether they were supportive towards the client or protective. A third possibility was allowed for, namely parents whose attitudes could be described as *conflict-ridden*.

Centres might, theoretically, contribute to home-based networks by offering enhanced opportunities to complement existing networks or compensation for deficiencies or limitations in existing networks. Centres might also respond to types of parental attitudes by offering strengthening of parental support or re-educative experiences to overcome the consequences of overprotective parental attitudes. Thus the following questions were asked:

1. **If a network was self-contained and the parents were protective.**

    Did the centre offer enhanced opportunities through extended centre-based networks and new activities? Did relationships with staff and others at the centre offer re-educative experiences of less protective, and more supportive, attitudes?.

2. **If a network was self-contained and the parents were supportive.**

   Did the centre offer new opportunities? Did it consolidate the support already available at home?

3. **If a network was embracing and the parents were protective.**

   Did the centre offer a network and activities which complemented, rather than competed with, what was available at home? Did relationships at the centre offer re-educative experiences in favour of less protective, and more supportive, attitudes?

4. **If a network was embracing and the parents were supportive.**

   Did the centre consolidate and facilitate what was available from home rather than compete with it?

These ideas suggested extremes which might not necessarily be the most desirable for the client's development. For example, everyone needs a measure of protection as well as support. Hence we talk about *over-protection*, meaning that the balance is tipped too much in favour of protection, taking into account the client's age, vulnerability and the realities of the outside world. In some instances though, parental attitudes might not be considered to be protective enough and in this case the centre might try to compensate or re-educate by offering a more secure environment and appropriately protective, as well as supportive, attitudes.

We also needed to be able to answer the question *protective* or *supportive* attitudes in relation to what? The research broke down the assessment of parental attitudes by looking specifically at domestic self-management, allowing the client to make new friends, engaging in a wider range of activities, sexual awareness, future accommodation and residential needs and taking on responsibilities.

The table below shows the extent to which parental attitudes varied in relation to specific topics in cases where the researcher felt there was sufficient data on which to base a judgement.

| | Number of Cases | | |
Topic	Supportive	Protective	Other*
General attitudes:	58	14	9
Specific attitudes:			
Domestic self-management	55	14	10
Making new friends	64	7	10
Engaging in a wider range of activities	71	6	5
Using public transport on own	32	34	5
Sexual awareness of client	14	22	12
Future residential needs	32	23	12
Taking on responsibilities	38	18	10

* Includes parental attitudes categorised as conflict ridden

It will be seen that parents' attitudes were most inclined to be supportive in promoting domestic self management, making new friends and engaging in a wider range of activities. They were inclined to be much less supportive in encouraging the client to use public transport and somewhat less supportive in relation to the client's future accommodation or residential needs. Supportiveness in handling the client's sexual awareness was difficult to assess. It was sometimes a taboo subject but in this respect attitudes also tended to be protective more frequently than they were supportive.

Parents are often thought by centre staff to be over-protective. Use the list of items in the Table to think more carefully about this.

Are parents' attitudes changing – i.e. are there any general differences between parents of younger service-users now compared with in the past, or with parents of older service-users?

A large majority of home-based networks were regarded as embracing. The figures were as follows in cases where the data made it possible to make an assessment:

Clearly embracing	32
Tendency towards embracing	32
No clear tendency	17
Tendency towards being self-contained	2
Clearly self-contained	3
Total	**86**

The decision of parents to send their sons and daughters to day centres itself represented a degree of outreach towards being embracing.

We look below at three different types of home background and in each instance ask what contribution the centre made in enhancing the quality of life at home.

1.   A self-contained network with protective parents

2.   An embracing network with a protective parent

3.   An embracing network with supportive parents.

Example 1 – May, self-contained network with protective parents

May was in her late twenties and lived at home with her parents. During the first monitored fortnight there were only two visits from home (other than to the centre) and during the same period she had two visitors at home. The contacts outside home were a special club, relations and parents' friends. Significant activities recorded at home included TV, radio and records, exercise and looking after the dog.

During the second monitored fortnight, about a year later, there were slightly more contacts at home. There were three visits out and three visitors came to see her at home. The main contacts were unchanged but there were more contacts with relations. Home-based activities were largely unchanged except that they now included knitting.

The only significant place outside the home identified by the parent and client was the special club, that is a club for other disabled people. Two significant people were identified and they were both relatives. The only enrichment to be identified from these contacts was the opportunity to play with a dog belonging to a relative.

The client appeared to be almost in prison at home. The mother did not believe that the client could, or should, learn new skills. She regarded the client as a child.

What was the centre doing about this situation? There were four visits out from the centre during the first monitored fortnight – to a cafe, for shopping, swimming and sports. Activities during this period which were recorded by the client as significant were domestic, educational activities, music and drama, bingo and discussions. During the second monitored fortnight, the visits from the centre were similar. The client recorded fewer activities as significant – these were diaries (for our research!), exercises and hygiene.

Staff were concerned with a wider range of activities. Six staff objectives were categorised as *developmental*, three were *task related*, two were oriented to daily living and one was categorised as a *social* objective. (For an explanation of these categories, see Chapter Four.)

In this case, the centre staff were aware of the problems for the client at home and the difficulty the parents had in accepting that the pursuit of the developmental and daily living objectives at the centre were worthwhile. They felt it important to work with the parents and, by the end of the research, it had been recognised that this entailed a degree of confrontation. There was also evidence that the centre was trying to compensate for the lack of a wider network at home by programming visits from the centre.

In general, this centre recognised client needs in accordance with the theoretical concepts we have suggested. In this case the network was self-contained, parental attitudes were protective and the centre response combined a compensatory enlarged centre-based network to incorporate activities not undertaken at home with re-educative centre experiences. These were described by one member of staff as being aimed 'to get her to involve herself with other people'. Other staff referred to her need for confidence and independence.

Example 2 – Linda, embracing network with a protective parent

Linda, also in her late twenties, lived at home with her mother and brother. She had a rich variety of activities and contacts at home. The parents said at the start of the study, 'She has a good active social life and the centre does not offer more than she would have at home', adding that 'Maybe Linda should stop going. She is not learning very much.' The mother was also concerned about Linda being injured as a result of fights with other clients at the centre.

During the first monitored fortnight, Linda's home network was further extended by a week's holiday in London. Afterwards the mother commented that this gave her greater confidence. In spite of the opportunities Linda enjoyed at home, the parents' attitudes were, in many ways, protective. Most things were done for her at home and she was escorted wherever she went. The parents seemed to have some conflicting attitudes about Linda making new friends. On the one hand they tended to see Linda's long-term future within the family and there was an emphasis on family relationships. On the other hand they were supportive in enabling Linda to engage in wider activities which involved normal people. The mother commented, 'Linda is not typical of a handicapped person because her friends are normal'. This applied especially within church activities which featured prominently in the life of the family.

The second monitored fortnight showed that Linda had a similar pattern of life when she was at home for the full period and not on holiday. She attended a special club for other disabled people which, to some extent, contradicted the mother's earlier comment about her mixing with normal people. However, there were many other opportunities for normal mixing within the church. Relations and family friends continued to play an important part.

The research allowed up to three nominations for the most significant places and people during each fortnight studied. In this case, the father (who answered for Linda) used the maximum allowed. Important places were the church, the church mission and the shops. The important people were all relations. The main benefits identified from these relationships were in terms of affection.

What was the contribution of the centre? Linda only attended for two days during the first monitored fortnight. Even this was enough to show that her activities were somewhat restricted, with contract work featuring prominently. Linda regarded the centre as the place she went to for work.

Changes occurred at the centre between the first and second monitored fortnights. Senior staff changed and there was an attempt made to focus more individually on Linda's needs and to broaden the base of her activities. By this time the mother had also become more positive in her views about the centre. She recognised that her daughter was learning something there – her comprehension was improving. She attributed this to the new staff. She also referred to a particular friend Linda had at the centre who was a client with greater disabilities. Linda herself when asked what she would change at the centre if she could, said 'More going out on buses.'

There was an emphasis on social objectives, usually expressed in such terms as *participation in groups*. This would seem to have been duplicating the opportunities Linda already had at home without adding anything. Something would only be seen to be added if there was evidence that the centre recognised the protective aspects in the close, if embracing, family life at home. She needed the opportunity to do things but essentially to make her own friends and do some things by herself. She had, apparently, the opportunity to do this with a more disabled person. But the parents had rightly emphasised the importance of her mixing with normal rather than disabled people.

Example 3 – Bert, embracing network with supportive parents

Bert, in his late twenties, lived at home with his parents and brother. He had close contact with a lot of relations, having come from a large family where all but one of his brothers and sisters had left home. He was also involved with his family in various special clubs. There was little change during the second monitored fortnight except that the network showed that the family had embraced even more clubs and special activities.

Bert had Downs Syndrome. He had good self-management skills although he was not always too well physically. His daily living skills were quite good as well, the only major difficulty being in using money. Nevertheless he travelled by public bus to get to the centre as well as in the family car for home activities and special buses for some of the clubs he attended. He could also read and write.

The parents' were supportive in almost all respects but this had not always been the case. The mother was aware that she had needed to overcome her previous protective attitudes. 'I never thought he'd be able to go on a bus on his own.' The parents said they would like to allow Bert more independence but they did worry a little about this. For example when they went out to a dance they tended to take Bert with them not because he wanted to go but because they did not like to leave him behind.

Three important places were named, all of them clubs. The three important people named included his brother, his sister (both living away from home) and a family friend whom he had met on holiday.

The important relations introduced Bert, in turn, to other members of their own families. Similarly the holiday friend was important because Bert had been introduced to his friends.

Centre activities recorded by Bert during the two monitored fortnights showed things that he considered important such as domestic activities during the first fortnight and printing work during the second. In fact his main activity at the centre, which was closest to the work model, was working at the printing press.

As one would expect with parents who were both embracing and supportive, there were quite high expectations which were not always fulfilled. The parents had made detailed criticisms about the centre in the past but even greater criticisms of previous centres Bert had attended. Here at least Bert seemed to be thoroughly enjoying himself and the activities at the centre probably gave him a sense of importance. In insisting, as the centre did, that Bert travel independently it can be said that the centre was extending the potential support offered by the parents and indeed extending and exploiting the potential of the network.

Was so much involvement in special activities the best way to achieve the centre's claim to lead to outside employment? Bert himself did not envisage ever leaving the centre. So far as he was concerned, he was at work already. The fact that he travelled independently perhaps made this more real. He stressed that going by bus was 'no problem at all'.

CHAPTER THIRTEEN

Staffing Issues

1. STAFF–TRAINEE RATIOS

Most local authorities in 1985–7 had policies designed to stand-
ardise the numbers of day service staff in relation to the numbers
of clients on the register, or in some cases the capacity of the centre.
Ratios were usually 1:8 or 1:9 (staff:clients) with more generous
allowances in the case of special care units or other specialist
centres such as the work centre. However, the research found that
the actual ratios varied from centre to centre.

Ratio of Staff to Clients

Centre	Ratio
10	1:13.3 (part-time attendance)
11	1:7.5
12	1:3.9 (with special care unit)
13	1:7.0
14	1:5.4 (work centre)
15	1:8.0
16	1:7.0
17	1:7.7
18	1:6.6
19	1:7.5
20	1:8.6
21	1:3.3 (new centre)
22	1:6.9 (with special care unit)
23	1:6.3
25	1:4.0 (not including allowance for follow-up work)

It will be seen that the numbers of staff varied very considerably from centre to centre, even taking into account the centre size. The different posts and whether they entailed, officially or unofficially, direct contact with clients, also varied very considerably. Some centres used trainees from youth training schemes (YTS) or other volunteers to help to make up perceived deficiencies in the numbers of staff, especially where individualised attention was considered to be important.

Based on the comments of staff and our own observations, individualised attention was not possible for any ratio greater than 1:4 (staff to clients). This figure allowed staff to be deployed flexibly so that some members could be given individual 1:1 or 1:2 attention while others were temporarily managing larger groups, depending on the activities pursued.

The importance of individualised attention and staff not looking after groups larger than two or three particularly applies to activities outside the centre such as shopping or visits into the community if these are to have any significant meaning in terms of promoting normal contacts within the community. The following were some of the researchers' observations at that time which illustrate the variability and complexity of the use of staff at day centres.

> There were 13 people in the room, to one instructor. Although the group is large for an adult training centre, the instructor did not need to give a lot of help with knitting, as most of the people present seemed fairly competent. She did, however, have to help with things like casting on and off.

> In theory, Mrs S (the drama instructor) is assisted by two instructors. However, she was on her own during the morning because of the instructors having to cover other staff duties. During the morning there were 15 clients.

> There were about seven or eight women in the room and the two instructors. The men clients tend to be split between two staff, each taking a group of five or six clients. Both do woodwork tasks with them.

> Jessie (an instructor) said to me at one stage that she does not usually like taking as many as six clients out and would normally prefer just to take two clients at once. However, if

she only takes two this leaves too many people in the groups back at the centre. The walk was used by Jessie educationally, for example to teach crossing roads and learning the name of the local school.

There were two members of staff – the manager and his secretary – and one volunteer. There were about 28 clients. This was the lowest ratio of staff to clients I have seen in a swimming session and it seemed to give more freedom to the individual clients to make their own contacts and do their own thing. There seemed to be more social interchange than is usually evident at the centre itself. I mentioned this to the manager who agreed.

After coffee I accompanied the special needs group swimming at the special school. There were three staff, plus myself and two clients. A third client usually comes but had been sick. One client who went in is a great fat lad. It required the two female instructors full-time to manage him, getting him ready to go in the water and then lifting him from a stretcher into the rubber tyre.

Would any of the above situations be likely to be different as far as staffing is concerned today? If so, in what ways? Has the staffing, as a resource to clients, improved during the past year?

---

2. STAFF QUALIFICATIONS AND BACKGROUND

We interviewed all the staff at all the centres in the sample, from managers, deputies and instructors to cleaners. We also interviewed visiting staff, other part-time staff and volunteers if they received allowances. This gave us a total sample of 221 people who would be seen by clients, in one way or another, as fulfilling a staff role. Apart from the 14 managers (one of the 15 centres did not have a manager), there were 11 deputies, 98 instructors including 2 teachers or lecturers, 5 visiting professionals, 9 regular volunteers and 84 others.

Out of the total of 221, 145 (66%) were women and 76 (34%) men. Taking managers, deputies and instructors alone, gender sex ratio was slightly more evenly balanced – 58% were women and 42% men.

At that time, 5 staff members had the CQSW, 6 had the CSS (social work qualifications), 19 had teaching qualifications, 11 had the DDTMH (a basic qualification for this work, no longer in existence), 18 had nursing qualifications and 42 had trade qualifications. Fifty-five claimed to have other qualifications which ranged from shorthand and typing to art. Seven had dual professional qualifications. Seven staff had relevant degrees. Of the 42 who had trade qualifications, one also had the CSS.

We also asked staff about their work experience background. Of the present staff at centres, a preponderance of both qualifications and background experience were in trade and industry.

Out of the 123 managers, deputies or instructors, 11 (9%) had the CQSW or CSS qualification.

> *To what extent have these profiles of staff features changed? What is the ratio of male/female and qualified/unqualified in your centre today?*

3. STAFF ROLES

A number of instructors, as they were called in 1987, wanted more responsibility. For example some said,

> Instructors should have more responsibility for what they do and should be allowed to take team decisions. They should be made team conscious.

For some staff this issue was linked with the need for more money. As one instructor put it,

> Our own role is changing too quickly anyway without enough planned thought going into the increased amount of responsibility we're getting. We're no longer overpaid given the drastic changes and decision making being placed upon us.

Some instructors felt they should be (and with some models of practice already were) working more in the community including home visits. Within the social care model this was linked with 'more caring, more social skills oriented, more working in the community'. Another instructor (at the same centre) wanted 'more outside centre activities at home, particularly for more independent people where numerous key workers are involved but not instructors'. When undertaking this, several instructors said they needed 'more management back-up, guidelines, structure and team planning'.

Similar views were echoed by several managers. At another Social Care Model centre, the manager said,

> The job has changed since years ago. There should be more time spent outside the ATC. As counsellor and field social worker, you have to operate in many ways.

Another manager, also from a Social Care Model centre, called for

> more outreach – operating out of the centre, possibly acting more as consultants and advisors to parents and outside agencies, organising specialised training input for specific situations possibly on a modular basis.

The manager of a Further Education Model centre saw the ideal role of the instructor in a model more oriented to the resource centre. Here the role of the staff would be 'to go out and make contacts in the community and use social networks'.

Another theme was in favour of retaining specialist roles for some instructors or other staff within a team setting. Some instructors, for example, called for much clearer guidelines about their work area and wanted a more systematic programme to follow through while still allowing for flexibility to meet people's individual needs. One manager in a Social Care Model centre pointed out the need to recognise such specialists as PE instructors, teachers, and music teachers, but also 'the need to be flexible to meet all the needs of clients and instructors'.

The need for different roles was linked by some staff with a need for greater clarity of role. We need a 'better job description'.

How far have these various points about staff roles and better job descriptions now been addressed?

Staff favoured the key worker idea. There were two aspects to this. First, development of key worker roles in working with clients within centres. During the research several centres already had such a system operating. One centre called them tutors. The key worker had the responsibility for managing the individualised learning programme for each client.

Second, some saw this as leading logically to the assessment of the client's needs in the light of home circumstances as well as in implementing individualised policy for each client using resources outside the centre itself. It involved linking with other agencies, raising the question of how the role of the instructor related to the role of the specialist field social workers then being appointed in some areas to undertake some of these tasks. One view was that the instructor should do this, that there should be a social worker *cum* instructor more in contact with the client's living circumstances and problems, i.e. a key worker's role. Another view was that the instructor, more modestly, should have a key worker role in being involved with other agencies such as the social worker, home help, community nurse rather than being the manager dealing mainly with them. One of the centres using the Throughput Model had begun to move in this direction during the research. Most of the staff welcomed it warmly:

> We have changed because of the key worker. A good thing for all concerned. It gives a better insight into the clients you are working with.

Another staff member said 'there's no saying it isn't a good thing' while another recognised it meant 'more social work'. The manager of this centre saw the development of the key worker role outside in working with families and the community as part of a wider vision:

> To develop a strategy we must emphasise the developmental function of our work – to give hope to instructors and their sons and daughters, as well as to benefit clients directly...so many people have a dreadful view of Adult Training Centres. Therefore these centres should not be seen in this context. Integration is the key to developing this service. We need the key worker concept to develop this issue more in the future outside the four walls of the centre.

The fact that this vision for the future was held amongst some staff before the publication of the Griffiths Report (1988) or any other influential official thinking and prior to the National Health and Community Care Act of 1990, illustrates how advanced some aspects of ideas about care in the community were so far as people with learning disabilities were concerned at that time.

Most staff and many managers at centres suggested that they had inherited out of date ideas about staff roles and staffing needs. This inheritance incorporated a mixture of rigidity and non-specificity. For example, staff ratios were traditionally calculated on the basis of one instructor spending a given amount of time with a group of clients for activities which were not defined except in terms of occupation or training. In the changed climate of ideas, managers were having to employ their ingenuity to pursue policies in line with one or more of the models of practice, using the staffing resources they had.

Both staff and managers expressed two contradictions about the situation. Firstly, staff were expected to be increasingly trained but there was insufficient provision for secondment. Secondly, staff were expected to be able to take more responsibility, for example in fulfilling key worker responsibilities, without an appropriate increase in pay, especially for those whose qualifications were not recognised. One instructor who had come from industry told us he had enough income himself but he wondered how the other instructors managed to bring up a family with what was very low pay compared with industry.

References

The Griffiths Report (1988) *Community Care: Agenda for Action.* London: HMSO.

CHAPTER FOURTEEN

Support for Carers

Over 60 per cent of parents welcomed, and expected, respite from care when their sons or daughters were attending day centres. The respite function was extended when centres also arranged holidays and outings.

Support for carers is a broader notion than respite – although respite or relief is an important aspect. Respite is especially important when carers are supporting people with multiple, severe or profound disabilities or those whose behaviour causes stress or damage.

Beyond respite, we wanted to find out how far the centre provided a resource to carers in terms of understanding and advice. More generally, how far did attendance at the centre promote the wellbeing and morale of the carers by demonstrating that things can be learnt? At some centres studied in the research parents were won over to believing in the possibility of progress. 'I never thought I would live to see the day when Jimmy would be able to…' was typical of comments made on several occasions.

> *Focusing on the needs of carers, as well as clients, has been given a boost in recent years with the implementation of the community care legislation. Do you recognise this as a legitimate aim for your day service? What do you understand by the term respite?*

Respite implied that carers were relieved of anxiety. It did not simply mean that they were relieved of the physical presence of their sons or daughters. They needed to know, as one parent put it that 'she gets training' because this 'relieves us of worry'. Or as another parent said 'I'm more at ease, knowing he's happy there'. Some parents wanted the respite function of centres to be more openly acknowledged. The issue of when centres are open was relevant here.

Practice in 1985–7 varied from a pattern of opening and closing incorporating from up to six weeks' holiday in the year to all the year round opening – apart from Christmas, New Year and local holidays. We asked parents whether the times centres were shut presented problems. Out of 137 parents who answered the question, 20 (15%) said there were problems and 91 (66%) said there were no problems. The remainder (19%) gave other answers.

Comments from parents who acknowledged their dependence on centres to fulfil a respite function included the following:

- I don't know what we would do without it.

- We wouldn't manage to do our work at all.

- We do get relief. You couldn't do without them but that is not as important as being there for the training.

Some parents acknowledged the value of respite in their particular circumstances. One parent said 'More so now as I'm getting older'. Another drew attention to the fact that she had two handicapped sons. Another pointed out that in the case of someone in a wheelchair 'Some parents need this'.

In general, as one parent put it 'If parents have handicap all the time, they can get frustrated'. Some clients told us that if they have their parents all the time, they could get frustrated! 'There's one thing I like about the centre', said one client, 'that is getting you out of the house'.

One staff member said, 'Centres do relieve parents. It is important that parents are relieved. It is important for parents and for the child as well'. Another referred to the caring role of the centre which extended to the parent. However, another staff member pointed out that although parents needed a break this 'should not be the aim of the centre. Too many parents use us as baby-sitters'. Another pointed out that respite to parents may be a by-product 'though as you make them (i.e. the clients) more independent, you will be relieving parents'.

Example of a Single Parent Family – Mary and her daughter, Jane

This was a single parent family where the mother worked full-time. Jane, the daughter, had a younger brother who was in full-time employment. The mother – Mary – said, 'I can work full-time but I would not be happy about leaving her all day at home alone'. However, she was not over-protective. Jane's network showed 14 home-based group activities, including nine mainly with other disabled people and five with non-disabled people. Jane engaged in 14 solo activities. In the follow-up discussions the significant activities outside the home were named as bingo, disco and doing grandfather's shopping. The significant people named included a personal friend, a family friend and a relation. The first two of these scored highly for all the relationship qualities studied, that is they were helpful to Jane instrumentally, in terms of access to others, emotional support and offering opportunities for reciprocal help. The third, who was the grandfather, was significant in offering opportunities for reciprocal help. The evidence showed that Jane enjoyed a rich life outside the home, apart from centre attendance.

There were, however, visits to the home only from one person, namely the client's friend. Life within the home may have been somewhat restricted. Significant activities named by the client were hygiene, domestic activities and watching TV.

The centre was closest to the social care model. The activities and staff objectives for a monitored fortnight were as follows:

Activities	Objectives
Art	Enjoyment
Kitchen duties	None (definitely stated)
Computer studies	To improve and learn new skills
Technical College*+	
Graduating from College	Confidence from having completed course
Stuffing toys	To improve skills
Garden	Enjoys it Keeps her busy
Chopping sticks*	To keep her busy No choice

Activities	Objectives
Contract work*++	To assess ability to do outside job, possibly outside employment To improve skills
Make-up*	To improve self confidence. She does have sexual awareness
Walk*	Social awareness To develop social skills Integration Communication Using community facilities and resources
Talk on fire prevention	Increasing awareness of dangers in the home To improve skills To increase knowledge of preventive measures
Physical education	To improve skills Encourage keenness Confidence – she does participate in other sports

Key

*   Major activity – at least 2 full days or equivalent during monitored period

**   Main activity – at least half the time during monitored period

+   Activity described as *very important* by staff

++   Activity described as *crucially* important by staff

Her mother could not manage Jane at home all the time. Perhaps the feeling was mutual. If the life within the home was somewhat restricted, Jane was probably as much in need of respite from the home situation as her mother was.

Jane was of relatively high ability and attended a course at technical college which happened to be completed during the monitored fortnight. Activities and objectives at the centre fell into two groups. Attendance at technical college and efforts to assess the client's potentiality for outside employment appeared to be specifically directed. If the client could find employment this could offer an alternative means of attaining respite. Another group of activities at the centre, however, appeared lacking in direction and were little more than occupation. Thus the garden and chopping sticks (a major activity) 'kept her busy'. One would have thought alternative means of promoting outside employment could have been considered, such as outside work experience.

Single parent families are one group likely to be particularly dependent on the provision of respite care. From this case it can be seen how important it is that this should not be regarded as the single or over-riding objective otherwise the client would tend to be given nothing more than activities aimed at occupation. On the other hand, if the centre's aims were directed towards the client's future elsewhere, she would have a lot going for her.

How do you square the need for a single parent to have respite with the needs of the client? What objectives would you have today in this kind of situation whether short or longer term?

CHAPTER FIFTEEN

General Conclusions – The Ways Forward

The research during 1985–7 evaluated seven possible models, or approaches, to practice. Each of them had strengths and weaknesses.

1. THE WORK MODEL

This had the attractiveness of simple objectives, namely to prepare people for work or work experience. Through work day service users could gain dignity and independence. The centre closest to this model was in many respects impressive. It had the highest rate of throughput (30%) for all clients during the research period (though not all of this throughput could be described as necessarily positive). Despite the difficulties of the current economic situation, open and sheltered employment and work experience placements were found. There were some signs, however, that the credibility of finding employment was difficult to sustain, especially for older clients.

The weakness of the work model was that it benefited younger people with relatively mild disabilities rather than older people with greater disabilities. Another weakness was that aims related to the client's home circumstances were neglected. There was no line of communication between centre and home which was clearly recognised and used. There is an argument that a work training placement should be 'realistic' – people have to recognise that employers expect their employees, disabled or not, to accept legitimate discipline and instructions and not to be thinking just of their own personal needs. Yet, to sustain this approach, home situations have to be taken into account.

2. THE SOCIAL CARE MODEL

Size was an important issue for this model. The aims were similar but the methods were very different. Issues included whether standard routines could be avoided in larger centres and whether spontaneity and a close knowledge of the individual circumstances of each client and their parents could be maintained. Another issue was whether details of the clients home-based networks were used adequately. The catchment area could also be related to size and the foregoing especially applied to smaller centres with a neighbourhood catchment area.

Whatever their size, these centres had moved slowly with the times in terms of the historical tradition of day centres in Britain. Their orientation was to the ethos of social work day care services in general – namely, to focus on the individual needs of each client in providing social activities and an understanding of social needs. The success or otherwise of the outcomes in these terms varied. They were all good at providing social activities. They were reasonably good in meeting the needs of parents in terms, for example, of respite – and they recognised that some clients also needed to get away from their homes for part of the day.

The centres varied in the extent to which they made use of the resources of other agencies and departments. However, it is in terms of the specific outcomes derived from concrete aims such as promoting more independent forms of living, achieving positive throughput and contributing in some explicit way to the enrichment of a client's network, that these centres were least impressive. Some of these aims involved clients and staff getting out beyond the four walls of the centres and establishing links with other agencies in ways which were unfamiliar to them. The result was that instead of promoting integration into the community, which they claimed to do, centres were sustaining a segregated life; albeit often a happy one, for the clients they served. This was less true for the smaller than for the larger centres.

3. THE FURTHER EDUCATION MODEL

The ideas behind this model of practice were relatively recent and the potentiality of the model itself may not have been realised, for different reasons, in the centres selected. Even so the findings in terms of outcomes for the more tangible measures, especially in terms of what clients learnt, were superior to the outcomes for the centres closest to the social care model. This educational model had the advantage of being specific in its objectives without the rigidity or restrictions of objectives associated with some of the other models. It was also demonstrated that this model of practice could cope more effectively with clients having profound disabilities than could the social care model.

4. THE RECREATIONAL MODEL

Like the work model, the recreational model had the merit of simplicity. Unlike the work model, it did not necessarily lead to greater integration into the community although it might lead to a more independent form of living. Sporting opportunities had been developing for disabled people of all kinds which could, theoretically, lead to greater contacts with non-disabled people. However, in the research there was no evidence of this happening to any extent. Bereft of this possibility, the recreational model could only be recommended on the grounds that clients enjoyed themselves, some gaining confidence and a sense of personal, bodily independence (especially if they had physical disabilities or sensory impairments). Parents (as at other centres) gained respite.

The recreational model stood for something which, while it should not be regarded as a complete or sole principle, nevertheless made an important contribution in strengthening other models. There were two reasons for this. First, not every person with a learning disability has physical disabilities and the development of their physical potential can be regarded as being of key importance in developing potential as a whole. Second, for clients who do have a physical as well as learning disability it was also important to address their physical needs. This was an argument for health care in its broadest sense including on the one hand specific provision for physiotherapy and other specialist treatments and on the other a general emphasis on healthy living.

The value of the recreational model was, therefore, in strengthening the viability of other models and in particular the further education model.

5. THE SHARED LIVING MODEL

The question for this model of practice, which the findings did not answer particularly hopefully, was whether shared living within a community was compatible with integration into the community outside. The findings of the research suggested that clients enjoyed themselves and gained in confidence but there were few tangible results in these terms and the extent of throughput was minimal.

One of the assets of the shared living model was that its inclusiveness of people with different kinds of disabilities to learn together meant that adults with profound and multiple disabilities were welcome. However being welcome and being in a position to benefit from being there, are two different things.

6. THE ASSESSMENT AND THROUGHPUT MODEL

The findings were fairly impressive for the two very different centres closest to this model, in promoting movement to more independent forms of living and contributing to patterns of living at home for example. The key characteristic was the notion of time-restricted learning programmes while still being free from any single notion of what *throughput* meant – it did not necessarily mean finding paid employment. The model exemplified the need for close liaison, if not a stage further in terms of integration, with other services and facilities.

There were two major limitations with this model. The first was its untested application to clients with very severe or profound disabilities. Second, there was a need for adequate resources to sustain a follow through service with clients after they had officially left. In this respect it could easily be argued (as for the further education model) that the assessment and throughput model had a natural match or merge with the resource centre model.

7. THE RESOURCE CENTRE MODEL

At the beginning of the research the resource centre model was more of an idea than actual practice so far as Scotland was concerned. It was only when we found a small urban-aided experimental project that we decided it would be possible to include it. During the period of the research, and since, the idea has developed and some of the other centres in the sample claimed to be moving towards this kind of practice. For our immediate purposes, however, we had only the one centre from which to evaluate it. The key distinguishing feature was routine part-time, instead of full-time, attendance. Part-time attendance encouraged making links between the client's home life and the centre. This was because the basic question had to be addressed of what the client did on days when he or she was not at the centre. We found that this centre had one of the more impressive records on throughput and the most impressive record of all the models in sustaining clients living independently. It was also impressive in terms of using other resources within the community.

COMBINATIONS OF MODELS

The question was asked whether there was single model of practice which could be inferred from the research findings combining the greatest strengths with the fewest weaknesses. The answer was that there was not, but three combinations or mixes of the models initially identified suggested a way forward. These three combinations had the potential to be developed into the recommended models of practice for the future:

1. **The Work Resource Centre Model** ecompassing specialist work preparation projects, but broadened to allow for an understanding of clients' home situations and, if necessary, coping with home-based influences which militate against the client finding work.

2. **The Further Education Resource Centre Model** which would be closely linked with colleges of further education, together offering social work and education resources.

3. **The Community Living Resource Centre Model** representing a combination of the assessment/throughput and resource centre models and their development within a network of community facilities, which could be expected to exercise normalising influences.

1. THE WORK RESOURCE CENTRE

The work resource centre would continue to put the main emphasis on promoting work experience and employment opportunities in the community rather than in providing work, occupation or work training on the premises. There would also be a recognised concern for the home circumstances of clients using the centre including working with parents.

Aims

(i)   To further opportunities for people with learning disabilities to find employment in normal settings.

(ii) To prepare and train people with learning disabilities to take up these opportunities.

(iii) To work with parents to ensure that people with learning disabilities are supported in employment.

(iv) To provide a local resource of information and advice to promote the employment of people with learning disabilities in the community.

Client Status

When clients first come to the centre they assume the status of a *potential worker*. They come to the centre for support and training in realising that potential.

Programmes and Activities

(ii) **Work Assessment** – where has the potential worker come from? What are his/her expectations, strengths and weaknesses? What goals need to be reached in order for the work potential to be realised? In what way can it best be realised in the local situation? What opportunities exist?

(ii) **Work Preparation** – what preparation is needed for a potential worker prior to his/her introduction (or re-introduction) into the work situation? Activities arranged will be in response to this question. For example they might include personal hygiene and physical fitness, basic training in safety and self protection, numeracy and literacy, language and communication. All these will depend on the individual's needs so that each worker will be pursuing an individualised learning programme. Group discussions also feature, helping potential workers relate to others in a group situation and gain support in understanding what they have to work at in order to attain their goals.

(iii) **Work Placement** – after the potential worker has been assessed as ready for some form of employment, the main effort is directed towards implementing this. A profile of the particular skills of each potential worker is matched with opportunities in open or sheltered employment or, if these are not available, work experience. Here the main focus of the work resource centre is outside the centre itself.

(iv) **Follow-Up and Support** – the centre is a resource for advice and support in sustaining the worker's progress in the work place and in dealing with any difficulties.

2. THE FURTHER EDUCATION RESOURCE CENTRE

This model combines the idea of the further education training centre with further education college provision for people with special needs. It also incorporates the notion of an educational resource centre offering a follow-up service for people who have completed courses.

Aims

(i)   To provide further basic and social education for adults with learning disabilities.

(ii) To encourage adults with learning disabilities to take advantage of normal further education classes whether part or full-time.

(iii) To co-ordinate with parents or other support people at home in realising the potential of adults with learning disabilities.

Client Status

Students

Programmes and Activities

Individualised programmes incorporating access to a wide range of opportunities within the college, together with special education appropriate for each student. This will include people with severe and profound disabilities as well as those with less severe disabilities. Normal facilities of a further education college will be supplemented in this respect by specialists from the health and social services including physiotherapy, speech therapy and occupational therapy. Further education is thus conceived in its broadest context of the maximum development of all aspects of the functioning of body and mind. Within this broad context there will be a specific application to students' daily living situations and continued support when a particular course at the college is completed. Not all activities will necessarily be held at the centre/college, however. There will be provision for the idea of staff serving as a resource to help students in their daily living situations.

Periods of attendance at the college would not necessarily be time-limited but specific courses would be. Thus any particular student will have a timetable comprising particular courses, following a given curriculum within a given period of time on sound educational principles.

3. THE COMMUNITY LIVING RESOURCE CENTRE

The community living resource centre is intended to contribute to the client's patterns of daily living both in general and more specific respects such as encouraging and facilitating clients in using normal community facilities and moving away from the parental home if they wish to do so; also enabling clients to prepare for situations where their main support people may become older and less able to help; helping to get recognition for the client's contribution to the community, whether voluntary or paid work or work experience. The resource centre also has a function in advising parents and clients on benefits and other resources that are available.

Aims

(i) To strengthen and support clients in daily living in the community.

(ii) To provide a resource to gain access to other facilities to this
     end.

Client Status
Service Users

Siting
Certain factors have to be taken into account such as immediate
access to town centre, shops and community facilities. Also there
must be easy access to public transport and the catchment area
should be small enough to enable clients to reach the centre independently.

Programme and Activities
The community resource centre is based on part-time attendance
and the focus of activities provided is to strengthen the capacity of
clients to make use of other facilities on the days when they do not
attend. Individualised programmes based on individual goal setting will derive from an assessment of clients' needs at home and
on what is required to strengthen their networks in daily living.
Activities will not necessarily take place within the centre. Staff
roles will include escorting clients in using normal community
facilities. On the other hand the centre would be seen as a place to
which clients could drop-in, at appropriate times, either for advice,
support or to meet friends. So far as its social activities are concerned, it should not necessarily be exclusively for people with
mental handicaps. They could, for example, bring their friends,
who might be considered non-disabled, into the centre.

RELATIONSHIP BETWEEN THE THREE MODELS
OF PRACTICE
These three models can be seen as complementary. In a large urban
area where specialisation of day care provision is feasible, a client
within the same catchment area of all three types of centre, could
move from the further education resource centre, which might be
the most appropriate placement for most school leavers, to one of
the others. A person already placed in work might move on from
the work centre to receive support at the community resource

centre. Older clients not expecting to find work (in the present economic situation at least) might most appropriately be at the community resource centre although the objective would be to wean them in turn from this to a regular programme of using normal community facilities and only using the resource centre as a back-up. What should be avoided is the idea of clients being fixed at any one particular centre for a long period of time.

In small towns and other areas where such specialisation of provision was not justified, smaller resource centres which combined functions should be encouraged. Combining of functions, however, should not be at the expense of losing the identity of purpose of each one.

THE FUTURE

Do day services have a future? At the time that *Day Care at the Crossroads* was published in 1988, two contradictory things were happening. The number of new day services was growing, yet the idea of day services was already being questioned. Some were arguing that day services would never be compatible with the need to help people with learning disabilities (at that time referred to as people with learning difficulties) integrate with 'ordinary' people in the community.

It can be argued that official policy with regard to day services is linked with policies relating to employment. Traditionally, training and occupation at day centres legitimised opting out of the labour market when work was regarded as a social obligation. All of that has changed! Work, for those able to obtain it, is a financial necessity and part-time work has increased for this reason.

Unemployment statistics are now presented in a way which restricts the definition to those eligible to claim unemployment benefit. This reinforces a notion that the social obligation is no longer to be in work but simply to avoid being classed as unemployed.

Between a common sense notion of having a *proper* job and being recognised as unemployed, there are nowadays a host of labels and possibilities, including low-paid part-time work, full and part-time education, training schemes or just not being counted. Day services lie somewhere in this gap. One positive consequence is that further education opportunities have also increased for people with learning disabilities and potentially could increase a lot more. However, with the new structure and marketing of further education, the continued attractiveness of students with learning disabilities to FE colleges is not always clear and the opportunities may vary, depending on the extent to which individual colleges are prepared to promote opportunities and commit resources.

Meanwhile, the movement for promoting integration in schooling has gained some, but not much, momentum. As with community care, integration in schools requires resourcing. So long as such opportunities are ambivalently seen by government as financially attractive options as well as an idealistic vindication of free market forces in a welfare system, their progress will be stifled at points where the money pinches. In theory, and to some extent in practice, integration experiences in schools should motivate carers, professionals and young adults with disabilities themselves, to push for better services for adults which support them in pursuing their opportunities in the community. Yet what would these opportunities be? Apart from further education which we have mentioned, what do the other options for non-employed ordinary youngsters offer those of their ex-school colleagues who are disabled?

Disability services are left, with others, to compete in the enterprise culture. There are opportunities, risks, hopes and disappointments in this process. There are winners and losers. The movement from long-stay hospitals has proceeded apace and brought with it demands for increased day-service provision as well as supported accommodation.

Society continues to spend a lot of energy, and some resources, defining and then responding to the misfit. Within the field of learning disabilities, the misfit is the person with so-called challenging behaviour. He (less often she) is a misfit – sometimes because they respond aggressively to the insufficient support and opportunities of standard provision that care in the community can afford.

The arrangements for care in the community should be used to help day services define their goals more carefully and convincingly. Day services should be more responsive to individual needs and accountable in terms of the idea of a provision that is purchased on behalf of the client. Within a purchased *package of care* there should be coherent links between day services, respite, specialist and domiciliary services. This is especially important for people with multiple disabilities, including clients with visual, hearing, touch and other sensory impairments. The basis for such a package is holistic community care assessment, taking into account the needs of carers as well as clients – or perhaps one should say the needs of the family household as a whole. (For a fuller discussion of these points see Seed and Kaye *Handbook for Assessing and Managing Care in the Community*, Jessica Kingsley 1994).

More attention is being given today to addressing the specialist needs of people with particular disabilities or impairments. This includes providing specialist day services provision and reflects a concern that people with learning disabilities who also have additional disabilities – for example, epilepsy, cerebral palsy or more rare syndromes – should not be neglected. The same is true for people with visual or hearing impairments (or both). Resources are available for some expensive services, though their availability varies in different areas.

There has also been a new investment in specialist equipment for some day services and more careful consderation to design issues when new centres are planned or old centres adapted. 'Multi-sensory' rooms are becoming fairly standard provision, for example, where clients with multiple and sensory disabilities are given particular attention. Products of the technological revolution are finding their way into some day services – not just computers and specialist educational software, but sophistated items such as sound beams.

Another development is the interest being shown by various alternative therapies and complementary medicine in meeting the needs of people with learning and multiple disabilities. For example, aromatherapy – already featuring in a few of the examples studied in 1985 – has become more common. Specialist therapies and, in particular, physiotherapy, speech and language therapy and occupational therapy, are in some areas slightly more accessible, partly because of a shift of emphasis from hospital to community care and partly because some centres (or individual families) can find the means to purchase their services.

However, more generally, people with learning disabilities are just one of many groups of second-class citizens struggling, with their carers (if they have them), primarily for survival. They may look from time to time as up a shaft from the bottom of an old mine, to something called *quality of life*. This sounds sweeter than *normalisation*. (What ordinary person talks of normalisation?)

The narrow challenge is, as always, to make the best use of mutual self-help, advocacy – call it what you will. This means linking, networking, across the boundaries of the old and the newer bureaucracies – the old departmental boundaries and the newer fiscal divisions induced by such notions as cost-centres. Accept the enterprise culture and exploit it, or at least make the best of it, for yourself, your family – and your day centre!

The broader challenge is to re-create, with the disadvantaged, a more humane quality of life for all of us. Day care is still at the crossroads, but the signposts have changed.

Suggested Further Reading

1. The British Institute for Learning Disabilities (BILD) has produced a series of learning materials for day service staff. *Have a Good Day* is prepared by Philip Seed and Jim Wood and the series is edited by John Harris. For details contact: BILD, Wolverhapton Road, Kidderminster DY10 3PP.

2. A more detailed account of Philip Seed's research in 1985–7 is contained in *Day Care at the Crossroads* (1988) published by Costello, Tunbridge Wells, Kent.

3. More case studies from the original research are to be found in Philip Seed's recently updated book *Day Services for People with Learning Disabilities* (1995) published by Jessica Kingsley, London and Bristol, Pennsylvania. The people studied have been re-visited ten years on.

4. The approach used in these case studies has since been developed and applied to assessment and care management more generally for practitioner purposes. See Seed, P and Kaye, G *Handbook for Assessing and Managing Care in the Community* (1994) published by Jessica Kingsley.

5. A detailed description of the methodology for studying social networks is contained in two further books. Practitioners should read Seed *Introducing Network Analysis in Social Work* (1990) published by Jessica Kingsley. Researchers should also read *Applied Social Network Analysis* (1987) published by Costello.

6. Philip Seed and colleagues are available for training and consultation. Write to: 70 Hay Street, Perth PH1 5HP

Models of Practice

The following are seven 'ideal types' of practice models identified during the early stages of the research and used as the basis for selecting centres for follow-up studies.

Features	The Work Model	The Social Care Model	The Further Education Model
Objectives	To provide work experience and where possible preparation for employment	To develop normal living potential, and social skills in family and community context	To provide continuing education To encourage assumption of adult responsibility
Methods	Work training Social skill	Social/Behavioural assessment Problem-solving individualised programmes	Group learning Classes Projects Ed. assessment
Assumptions	Society should provide employment for mentally handicapped people	Social work has a role in meeting individual and family needs	Society should allow slow learners to develop to their potential as adults
Staffing Implications	Craft/Industrial instructors – DRO Psychologists	CSS & COSW	Teachers Lecturers
Administrative Implications	'Trainees/ Workers' Centres industrially located Separation of special care	'Clients' Proximity to normal living situations Links with special housing	'Students' Location with access to FE Colleges and community facilities

The Assessment and Throughput Model	The Recreational Model	The Shared Living Model	The Resource Model
To channel people on to more appropriate (more normal) placements	To allow the person to develop a range of interest and activities	To provide a community within the ATC To break down staff/trainee barriers	To provide access to a wide range of normal facilities
Assessment Schemes developed outside centre short-term Intensive Training	Maximised choice Large range of activities Part-time attendance possible Contact when needed	Shared learning Shared residence/evening activities	'Open door' advertised Information on aids benefits etc. Family involvement
Society should allow for a range of options for MH people	MH people able to make choices about their lives and entitled to positive occupation leisure pursuits	MH people have a possible valued contribution to make to other people	Facility should be outward-looking to meet a variety of client and community needs
Assessors Instructors Linked personnel in facilities outside ATC	Instructors Craft Workers Community Workers Volunteers	Members	Mixed skills e.g. Welfare Rights Community Workers
Located close to range of community facilities	'Members' Links with local leisure facilities	'Members' possible links with philosophical movement Mixed groups e.g. physically and mentally handicapped	'Users'/ 'Visitors' Links with community groups

Index